THE

BREAK AWAY

MOVE

ROBERT S. FISH

ENTREPRENEUR · BUSINESS COACH · PRO ATHLETE · SPEAKER

THE

BREAK

AWAY

MOVE

IGNITE YOUR COMPANY'S CORE, ACCELERATE GROWTH, AND *CRUSH* THE COMPETITION

FOR CEOS, ENTREPRENEURS, AND LEADERS

Published by Advantage, Charleston, South Carolina.
Member of Advantage Media Group.

ADVANTAGE is a registered trademark, and the Advantage colophon is a trademark of Advantage Media Group, Inc.

Printed in the United States of America.

10 9 8 7 6 5 4 3 2

ISBN: 978-1-59932-598-9
LCCN: 2016954386

Book design by Megan Elger.

This publication is designed to provide accurate and authoritative information in regard to the subject matter covered. It is sold with the understanding that the publisher is not engaged in rendering legal, accounting, or other professional services. If legal advice or other expert assistance is required, the services of a competent professional person should be sought.

 Advantage Media Group is proud to be a part of the Tree Neutral® program. Tree Neutral offsets the number of trees consumed in the production and printing of this book by taking proactive steps such as planting trees in direct proportion to the number of trees used to print books. To learn more about Tree Neutral, please visit **www.treeneutral.com**.

Advantage Media Group is a publisher of business, self-improvement, and professional development books and online learning. We help entrepreneurs, business leaders, and professionals share their Stories, Passion, and Knowledge to help others Learn & Grow. Do you have a manuscript or book idea that you would like us to consider for publishing? Please visit **advantagefamily.com** or call **1.866.775.1696**.

TABLE OF CONTENTS

FOREWORD

I can't think of anyone more qualified to write about the BreakAway Move than Robert Fish. He has one of the most unique stories I've encountered. He is a man who has seen success at the highest levels in both business and professional athletics. More importantly, in the midst of experiencing such tremendous success against the odds, he is one of the most soft-spoken and humble men I have ever encountered.

Robert's story is far more compelling than the notable accomplishments he's achieved as a founder of four companies. His story includes becoming the first 40 year old to professionally compete in the National Championship as a mountain bike racer and is about setting outlandish goals, enlisting the wisdom of others, driving daily discipline, and being relentlessly resilient.

What I admire most about knowing Robert and his story is his quiet, selfless disposition. He is fixated on practically helping other entrepreneurs, CEOs, and their management teams realize their collective dreams in practical, actionable, and achievable methods. He has an impressive track record of helping CEOs and their teams scale up, improve alignment, gain freedom, and have more fun along the way.

The BreakAway Move draws interesting parallels between building a high-performance company and becoming a high-performance athlete with three key areas of focus: strengthening your core, discovering your BreakAway Move, and executing the plan—making the breakaway move stick.

As you dive into discovering your own BreakAway Move, you'll see common themes: aim high, build your core, separate from the pack, relentlessly execute daily, and, most importantly, an invitation to savor the journey in the process.

You'll see that Robert's view of achievement isn't just about hearing the roar of the crowd or standing on the winner's podium. It is about learning, growing, and overcoming the challenges of a hyper-competitive marketplace—and life— while fostering gratitude for being along for the ride with a valued team.

I hope the lessons highlighted in *The BreakAway Move* book will help you and your team win in the marketplace—and in life!

—Gary Frey

INTRODUCTION

In mountain bike racing, a breakaway move is a calculated maneuver designed to push the competition into the red zone. Once in the red zone, racers struggle to keep up, begin to burn out, or start committing handling errors, providing a moment of weakness where one can jump in and seize the lead. To capitalize on this moment, racers must have intimate knowledge of their competition, understand where their opponent is weak, carefully judge the timing, and be prepared to drop the hammer at just the right moment. When successfully executed, a breakaway move is exhilarating! However, as exciting as it can be, the breakaway move in and of itself does not ensure a win. With the right training, most racers are able pull away from the pack at one point or another. To reach the top of the podium, racers must execute a breakaway move *and* keep up the pace to maintain the lead. The win requires strategy and resilient execution.

Personally, I discovered the BreakAway Move concept through mountain bike racing, but the strategy is not unique to the sport. In hockey, the term describes a moment when an offensive player breaks away from the pack, speeds down the ice, and takes a shot on

> **PERSONALLY, I DISCOVERED THE BREAKAWAY MOVE CONCEPT THROUGH MOUNTAIN BIKE RACING, BUT THE STRATEGY IS NOT UNIQUE TO THE SPORT.**

goal before the opposing defenders can catch up with him. In basketball, it is when an unguarded offensive player runs down court to catch a pass with no defenders in the way, usually resulting in a game-changing dunk. The concept is present in several sports, because the message is universal. Whether you are applying the breakaway move in team or individual sports, or translating the strategy for use in business, the instructions are the same: identify your goal, develop a strategy, prepare for the moment, and execute your move.

I began racing mountain bikes at thirty-six years old, the age at which most pro athletes are planning their retirement. Like most boys who grew up in the 1980s, I grew up riding BMX bikes, and although I always enjoyed riding, I never thought seriously about racing professionally. Sure, the idea had crossed my mind a time or two in college, but my focus was elsewhere. While still in college, I started my first company. Following school, I continued my entrepreneurial journey, got married, and started a family. For me, mountain bike riding was a great way to stay fit and let off some steam. But everything changed in 2010, when, standing before a group of my peers at a local entrepreneur event, I said aloud, "I want to race mountain bikes professionally and compete in the mountain bike nationals."

Standing up and announcing a dream so big, so huge, so seemingly impossible, takes courage—massive amounts of it. The moment the words "I want to race mountain bikes professionally" left my mouth, I began to feel the pressure set in. Saying the words was just the first step. My goal was bigger than me and required a new way of thinking. After all, I was entering a sport where the average competitor age was on the low side of twenty; I, on the other hand, was just one year shy of the big four-zero. Against such overwhelming odds, I realized a win this big needed great training and a superior strategy. This decision to develop and follow a plan proved invaluable to my racing success. When I was sure I had reached my limit mentally and physically, coaching guided me through until I dug deeper, produced more, and fought my way to a ranking of thirteenth nationally. When I experienced two potentially career-ending injuries in the span of five months, it was clarity and vision that provided the motivation necessary to defy the prognoses of multiple surgeons. And when I faced a younger, more experienced group of competitors, it was a focused strategy and superior physical conditioning—developed through unique and efficient training—that helped me identify and execute my breakaway move.

WHEN I WAS SURE I HAD REACHED MY LIMIT MENTALLY AND PHYSICALLY, COACHING GUIDED ME THROUGH UNTIL I DUG DEEPER, PRODUCED MORE, AND FOUGHT MY WAY TO A RANKING OF THIRTEENTH NATIONALLY.

In June of 2012, while positioned at the mountain bike racing pro nationals starting line, I experienced an epiphany. My journey to becoming a pro mountain bike racer (huge goal), along with the experience of intense training, suffering injuries, learning from failures, and celebrating successes (the adventure), resulted in a win beyond anything I ever imagined—something I call an "Epic Win." Discovering this relationship between training and strategy helped me attain a seemingly impossible goal. But most importantly, the experience revealed to me a roadmap for success, both on and off the bike.

EPIC WIN

ADVENTURE   +   HUGE GOAL   =   EPIC WIN

Emboldened by my experience, I began to formulate a plan of leveraging what I had learned to help others professionally. Soon after nationals, I founded Insight CXO, a firm dedicated to helping company leaders and their teams learn and grow. Since August of 2013, we have helped countless organizations define their goals, implement a scalable plan, identify their BreakAway Move, and achieve their own Epic Win. My desire for this book is to help you do the same.

THIS BOOK AS YOUR COACH

Prior to founding Insight CXO, I started and led three successful companies. The experience gave me an intimate understanding of the unique pressures of leadership and motivated me to help entrepreneurs and company leaders avoid the pitfalls that plague so many businesses. For this reason, I structured Insight CXO with a coaching methodology rather than a consultant approach. Consultants design a plan and then leave you to execute the various layers on your own, whereas a coach walks side by side with you. Coaches are with you as you grind through every step, celebrate successes, and recalibrate after losses. A coach has a stake in the outcome and really cares about the result. CEO coaching benefits the entire organization, allows leaders to reflect on strategy free from pressure or deadlines, and creates an opportunity to gain much-needed perspective from someone outside the organization. Many of the most successful and admired business leaders have a coach! In fact, Bill Gates (Microsoft), Jeff Bezos (Amazon), and Eric Schmidt (Google) at one time all shared the same

> **I STRUCTURED INSIGHT CXO WITH A COACHING METHODOLOGY RATHER THAN A CONSULTANT APPROACH.**

coach, the late Bill Campbell. These men understood an accepted truth among professional athletes: If you want to take your game to the next level, you will need a great coach.

The focus of this book is to share with you the roadmap to success through which I guide and coach my clients. Whether you are a small, midsize, or large company—or even if you are a thirty-nine-year-old dreamer wanting to achieve bigger-than-life goals—I want to help you understand the foundational principles and strategies necessary to break away from the pack and achieve your Epic Win! I am looking forward to the journey and hope you are too.

Chapters 1 & 2—Core Purpose & Core Values
Your company's core consists of the purpose and values that you consider immovable and unshakable. Your core defines the character of your business, and a strong core is essential to your organization's health and direction. In the first two chapters, we discuss **how to identify your company's core values, how best to integrate your core values into the culture, and methods for employing core values and core purpose operationally**.

Chapter 3—Epic Win

For your company to do something great, it is critical that everyone have a shared vision of success and a clear understanding of your Epic Win. Pursuing a huge, clearly defined goal inspires the team and results in a shared drive, from the frontline employees all the way to the boardroom. In Chapter 3 you will discover **what defines an Epic Win and how to create your own.**

Chapter 4—Winning Teams

Once you have identified your Epic Win, you need the support of a strong team to help you achieve it. Chapter 4 exposes **the importance of strong players, the necessity of defined roles, and how best to align your team's efforts.**

Chapter 5—The BreakAway Move

Now that you have defined your core values, identified your Epic Win, and surrounded yourself with a strong team, it is time for strategy. In this chapter, you will learn about **the BreakAway Move strategy, a calculated maneuver designed to accelerate you past the competition.**

Chapter 6—BreakAway Move Development

It is critical that you and your team develop a strategy to increase top-line revenue, one best suited for your unique structure and needs that will help you achieve your Epic Win. Chapter 6 guides you through **your BreakAway Move development by focusing on top-line revenue, surveying your competition, engaging in brainstorming exercises, and creating a clear action roadmap.**

Chapter 7—Selecting BreakAway Moves

With technology developing at a breakneck pace and new competitor threats looming around every corner, it seems increasingly difficult to stay ahead of the pack. In Chapter 7 you will determine your **best BreakAway Moves to crush your competition!**

Chapter 8—Execution

Becoming a successful professional athlete, at any age, does not happen overnight. It requires a fanatical dedication to planning and preparation while also pacing yourself to avoid burnout. Your business's growth strategy should be approached in the same way. In this chapter, you will discover the **strategic and tactical methods necessary to accomplish your Epic Win, one week at a time**.

Chapter 9—Resilience

Issues, setbacks, and constraints are inevitable, and how you and your team respond to them is critical. In Chapter 9 you will discover **how to be resilient during negative experiences and turn them into learning opportunities.**

Chapter 10—Start to Finish

Now that you have all the pieces in place, it is time to create the race plan for your company. In Chapter 10 you will **develop the process to implement BreakAway Moves within your own company.**

PART I

IGNITE YOUR COMPANY'S CORE

CHAPTER 1

CORE PURPOSE—FIND YOUR "WHY"

"When you're surrounded by people who share a passionate commitment around a common purpose, anything is possible."

—Howard Schultz, Starbucks

As I began serious training, I learned the best approach for both a breakaway move and an Epic Win is centered around building a strong core and developing an equally strong fitness base. Basically, this means being super fit from your knees to your mid-chest while also having a highly developed cardiovascular system. This core muscle group serves many purposes. At a basic level, it protects and contains the vital organs housed in the core while also making it possible for us to stand upright. Strong core muscles can ward off leg and arm fatigue for runners, effectively increasing their stamina and resilience. Pitchers draw on their core strength when commanding their arm and shoulder muscles to produce the nastiest curves, sliders, and fastballs. And in mountain biking—a sport requiring extreme amounts of power *and* endurance—the core is critical.

Just going out and riding your bike as hard as you can every time you ride does not result in peak performance—not even close. Think of fitness in terms of a pyramid; the pyramid can only be as tall and sturdy as the base allows. Essentially, a strong, well-developed base allows for a tall pyramid, and conversely, a weak base will result in a small, unimpressive structure.

For this reason, all mountain bike training plans begin with a "base period." This phase is comprised of long, slow miles on the bike coupled with strength training in the gym. This approach creates a platform upon which peak fitness may be achieved by layering on harder and more intense workouts throughout the year. The base period trains your body to burn fat, rather than sugar, as its primary fuel source during exercise. Fat, the more efficient fuel source, enables your body to handle long, intense workouts and races. Plus, the extra muscle mass will provide the power necessary to make your breakaway move and stay in front of the pack.

Creating healthy businesses also requires a strong core and developed base. But instead of muscle and cardiovascular fitness, they require a powerful *core purpose* (a company's reason for being, its higher cause, its heartbeat, its endless supply of energy) and clearly defined *core values* (intrinsic values that define the people and the company).

SECTION ONE: THE IMPORTANCE OF A STRONG CORE PURPOSE

While a company's vision statement explains its future purpose, a company's core purpose describes why it exists today. Why does your company exist? What is your organization's purpose? I am not asking what you do or what you sell; I want to hear *why you do what you do.* I want to discover what drives your organization. Your organization's purpose—your "why"—should be a powerful statement defining your company's *raison d'être,* or reason for being. My personal core purpose was and still is "pushing limits." It is why I became a pro athlete, why I started multiple companies, and why I am writing this book. At Insight CXO, our core purpose is "Helping entrepreneurs and their teams learn and grow." Our purpose provides clarity and guides our team toward what we should be doing and away from what we should not be doing. Every project we engage in and every client we take on should drive our core purpose forward.

Your company's core purpose should speak to you and your team's soul. It should inspire employees to get out of bed, go to work, and make the world a better place. This is a significant element in developing a strong core in any business. Without a strong and meaningful core purpose, it is much harder, if not impossible, to achieve peak performance. A solid core purpose creates a desire for teamwork, because it creates a sense of connection with a common belief. Although most of an organization's workforce is at the tactical level, people desire to be part of something bigger. Defining your company's core purpose and communicating it to all levels of your organization fosters a team dynamic that is likely to result in a more engaged and productive workforce. Having a strong core purpose is also a very powerful tool in attracting the right candidates to work for your company. Great organizations have a solid core purpose, and great employees are drawn to great organizations.

CREATING YOUR CORE PURPOSE: THE CORE PURPOSE DISCOVERY PROCESS

Defining your organization's core purpose is an essential first step in any business strategy. An organization must know why it exists before determining how it can allocate its resources. When working with clients who are struggling to define their purpose, I first ask them to tell me what it is they do. Simply put, I ask them to tell me the function of their organization. After the team has settled on their function, I then walk them through the *core purpose discovery process*. This process, also called *the five whys*, will help you define your core purpose and quickly incorporate it into your organization's operations.

DEFINE YOUR FUNCTION

First, think about what you do as a company, and ask your team to do the same. Consider your company's function in as broad and simple terms as possible. If you are in the accounting software business, you might say something like, "We deliver accounting software solutions." Don't be concerned if your answer appears generic or plain, as you are merely defining function at this point. As you work through this with your team, see if everyone has a similarly simple description of what the company does. You would be surprised how often team members come up with totally different descriptions. Although this happens often, it is important that you resolve the differences and agree upon a shared definition prior to moving on.

THE FIVE WHYS

Next, walk through the core purpose discovery process. Keeping the company's function in mind, ask the following questions:

1. Why is this important?

2.   Why does it matter?

3.   Why is this important?

4.   Why does it matter?

5.   Why is this important?

As you work your way through the questions, write down the responses. Amazingly, as the team settles on answers to each question, you will start to uncover the intrinsic value of your organization's function and will begin to see your purpose form. I encourage teams to lean into this process, but I also caution them from taking it too far. Although we want your organization's purpose to evoke emotion and inspire the team, it should also logically align with your company's function and explain why your company exists today.

COSTNER LAW—CORE PURPOSE EXAMPLE

Costner Law, founded by Josh Costner, is a firm focused on residential real estate transactions. It is one of the fastest-growing law firms, having landed on the Inc. 500 list and making multiple showings on local Fast 50 and Best Places to Work lists. Josh understands the importance of a healthy company culture, so on day one, he and I began the work of defining the organization's core purpose and developing strong core values. After going through the five whys process with the entire company (twenty people, at the time), we landed on "Make real estate transactions simple and smooth." This defined purpose gave the company clarity and direction in creating great experiences for their clients.

Two years later, Josh's firm had grown to sixty-plus employees, with multiple offices in three states. During our annual planning session, we circled back on core purpose to see if we really got it right and whether the core purpose still evoked a powerful emotional connection with the team. To reevaluate, the team decided to run through the five whys process once more, and the result was nothing short of magical. We transformed the original core purpose from "Make real estate transactions simple and smooth" to "Celebrate life's transactions." Costner Law Firm experienced great growth, and ultimately, their core purpose underwent the same. Think about the power and influence Costner's new and improved core purpose has on daily operations. Team members who had previously seen themselves as facilitating a process were now invited to celebrate in that process. How might someone approach their duties differently thinking in celebration terms rather than viewing themselves simply as a facilitator? How might this affect the reputation of the firm? Costner Law Firm is now one of the most referable law firms in the market. This is a perfect example of how language can have a dramatic impact on perspective. Buying a home is a huge life transaction, and Costner Law wants to do more than facilitate the transaction—they want to celebrate it!

To download the "Energy Secret – Core Purpose™" worksheet, go to: www.insightcxo.com/tools.
Also see Appendix A.

THE ENERGY SECRET – CORE PURPOSE™

WORKSHEET PURPOSE:

To identify what really gets the company motivated to accomplish great things. Answers the why we do what we do question.

DESCRIPTION STATEMENT "WHAT DOES YOUR COMPANY DO?"

_____

_____

1. WHY IS THIS IMPORTANT?

_____

_____

  2. WHY DOES THIS MATTER?

  _____

  _____

    3. WHY IS THIS IMPORTANT?

    _____

    _____

      4. WHY DOES THIS MATTER?

      _____

      _____

        5. WHY IS THIS IMPORTANT?

        _____

        _____

OUR CORE PURPOSE: _____

  Hints: _Keep this as a short phrase so it's easy to remember._
      You don't have to go 5 deep on the Why's. If #3 resonates, use it.
      Do this first in draft from and circle back until it feels right.

CHAPTER 2

CORE VALUES—FOUNDATION FOR PEAK PERFORMANCE

"Define what your brand stands for, its core values and tone of voice, and then communicate consistently in those terms."

—Simon Mainwaring

We discovered in Chapter 1 that creating a healthy organization requires developing a strong core. Businesses require a powerful core purpose and clearly defined core values. And while a business's core purpose describes its reason for being, an organization's core values are the intrinsic values that define the company and the people within it. Essentially, core purpose describes the company's mission, and core values explain how to achieve the mission. In this chapter, we will discuss core values and the role they play in building a healthy enterprise.

A company's core values should be a handful of rules that clearly define the character and culture of the business. In the best-selling book *Built to Last*, Jim Collins and Jerry Porras define core values as inherent and sacrosanct, meaning they can never be compromised, neither for convenience nor short-term economic gain. Patrick Lencioni, author of *The Five Dysfunctions of a Team*, defines core values as deeply ingrained principles that guide the company's actions and serve as its cultural cornerstone. Clearly defined corporate values can inspire organizations in times of success and in times of adversity. For many companies, their core values serve as decision guardrails, guiding organizations as they adapt to growth. As Roy E. Disney so wisely stated, "It's not hard to make decisions once you know what your values are."

Companies don't just have cultures, they *are* cultures. As a leader, you must work with your team to identify your core values, communicate them within the organization, and protect them in your daily operations. Serious athletes would never play a game without first setting forth rules and guidelines, but companies operate this way all the time! Without a strong foundation to build upon, most companies struggle to gain traction and never reach peak performance. But those organizations that take the time to invest in strong, inward-facing core values will have a clear advantage over their competitors.

In the book *Corporate Culture and Performance*, John Kotter and James Heskett found that core-value–driven organizations consistently outperform their non-core-value–driven counterparts. In fact, when comparing performance over ten years, the authors found that stock prices for core-value–driven organizations were twelve times that of non-core-value–driven organizations! Much like the pitcher drawing on his core to hurl a fast ball over the plate and the runner drawing upon their core to increase stamina, organizations with developed core values have the strength and stamina necessary to successfully execute BreakAway Moves and sustain their lead ahead of the pack.

Core values should be a part of your employee onboarding and training processes. They should be incorporated in your employee handbook so that everyone knows what they are. Your organization's core values should be worked into position descriptions and Role-Alignment Cards. Integrating your core values into your organization's screening and interview processes is a recipe for success and a great method to scale.

Solid and believable core values can help managers as they coach their teams through recognizing the right decisions and avoiding the wrong

ORGANIZATIONS WITH DEVELOPED CORE VALUES HAVE THE STRENGTH AND STAMINA NECESSARY TO SUCCESSFULLY EXECUTE BREAKAWAY MOVES AND SUSTAIN THEIR LEAD AHEAD OF THE PACK.

ones. For example, a clear set of core values can make it easy for a somewhat inexperienced junior manager to have a conversation with an employee regarding a behavioral issue. The core value functions as a safety rail guiding that junior manager through the situation, allowing him or her to say to the employee, "Hey John, we have a core value called 'consistency.' We think that being consistent and coming to work on time every single day and putting in a good, hard effort creates a better environment of teamwork. When you are late to work, it hurts the core value. Your team members can't depend on you. It affects production. So, let's talk about the core value of 'consistency' and what needs to happen so that you can start showing up for work on time."

Although simple, this example illustrates how easy it is for a manager to address a problem quickly by filtering it through the lens of the organization's core values. The opposite, less productive approach would be to personally attack the consistently late employee. Leveraging the core value is a kinder way to have the same conversation and sets the stage for a constructive outcome, a new behavioral direction, and improved employee compliance.

When identifying Insight CXO's core values (listed below), we kept it simple so that team members could easily set their direction and run their daily actions through the lens of our culture, asking themselves questions like the following: Does my action support being a lifelong student? Am I being inclusive? How am I impacting my clients and my company through my work? Am I doing the right thing? Am I resourceful? Am I finding a way?

----

1. **Be a Lifelong Student**—Never stop reading, learning, or being open to new ideas; be curious; investigate things; etc.

2. **Be Inclusive**—Leverage the power of collective intelligence. Actively seek others' opinions and insight. Engage others who are not like you.

3. **Make an Impact**—If you are going to do something, make it impactful. Leave it better than you found it. Create something special and enduring.

4. **Do the Right Thing**—Make the right decision, even when no one is looking. Put others before yourself.

5. **Find a Way**—Don't always take no for an answer. Find a way to navigate through life's issues and setbacks. Think outside the box. Find creative solutions. Use constraints as a motivation for creative solutions.

YOUR ORGANIZATION'S CORE VALUES

Core values should pervade all aspects of an organization. The management team needs to be intentional about how to create and support core values. When assisting companies in creating their core values, I walk them through a three-stage process. The first stage centers on identifying core values. However, if the organization enters stage one with a culture firmly in place, our mission is simply to reveal what is already there and refine the core value language. In stage two, we focus on writing descriptive paragraphs that explain the core values in detail. Then, in the last stage, we walk through expressing the core values within the company.

1 Identify

2 Describe

3 Express

STAGE ONE: IDENTIFY YOUR CORE VALUES

Ideally, you should have no more than five core values that define the character of the business. Any more than this and it becomes difficult for employees to remember the core values, let alone apply them in their daily objectives. Also, when developing or refining your company's core values, try to limit yourself to only one or two that are aspirational. Even when a value is aspirational, there should be at least a small handful of people inside the company we can look to and say, "These are the people who model that behavior." Having a tangible example to point to makes it believable, actionable, and easier to manage.

Although I prefer to focus on positive stories and tools as a means of identifying a company's core values, negative experiences can be extremely useful considerations in the process. It can be uncomfortable to discuss, but revisiting a negative employee experience may reveal red flags that were missed and address potential weaknesses in an organization's core values. Have you had a negative hiring experience within your company? What was it about a past employee, behaviorally, that really caused problems? Did you keep the employee on longer than you should have when he or she was clearly not performing? If so, why? Ultimately, your goal should be to create a core value filter that only allows those who align with your culture to permeate the ethos of your company. Examining past hiring failures is a necessary step toward designing a robust and effective core-value–driven hiring filter.

> **YOU SHOULD HAVE NO MORE THAN FIVE CORE VALUES THAT DEFINE THE CHARACTER OF THE BUSINESS.**

To help organizations begin the process of identifying their core values, I introduce them to a highly effective exercise called the "Mars Mission." This process, developed by Jim Collins, is both easy and fun! The exercise guides participants through five steps designed to help a company create or refine its core values.

MARS MISSION EXERCISE

1. Schedule a meeting or off-site planning session with your leadership team. I like to include as many people as reasonably possible in the process.

2. Set the stage for your team. Your company has been selected to send a small group of employees to Mars to establish a colony with the Martians. The Martians cannot speak

English (or any other language on our planet). What five to seven people would you send from your firm who best exemplify the core and character of the business? These are the kind of people you'd hire more of if you could find them.

3. Of the five to seven people your team has selected, what are the attributes or defining character traits one of each? Using sticky notes or a whiteboard, have everyone share their list of attributes.

4. Take the list of attributes and begin to create buckets of similar descriptions. You should end up with three to five buckets or categories that we will now consider your core values. Now, give each one of these buckets a name that best describes its contents.

5. To test your core values to see if you got them right, run each one through these three questions: a) Does this core value exist in the company today? b) Would we be willing to take an economic hit to defend this core value? c) Would we be willing to fire a repeat offender if he or she could not get in line with the core value?

Jim Collins and Jerry Porras, "Building Your Company's Vision," *Harvard Business Review*, September–October 1996.

After completing the exercise, you should have produced a list of attributes that describe your core values. Next, work collectively to compile your findings and then filter the group list through the three questions in step 5 of the Mars Mission exercise. As a reminder, your goal should be to arrive at three to five strong core values that will stand the test of time. Once you have your list, continue to review it and fine-tune the language every thirty days for the next three to six months.

1 Identify

2 Describe

3 Express

STAGE TWO: DESCRIBE YOUR CORE VALUES

Stage two of the core values creation process consists of creating descriptive paragraphs in support of each core value. *You will begin stage two prior to completing stage one.* As you and the team meet every thirty days to review the core values' language, simultaneously create the descriptive paragraphs for each core value. Aligning the stages in this way supports language consistency and promotes clarity.

1 Identify

2 Describe

3 Express

STAGE THREE: EXPRESS YOUR CORE VALUES

Once you have defined your core values, always be expressing them! Print your organization's core values on banners and display pictures that illustrate them in action. The core value message should be a visceral component of your company that is thoughtfully and professionally displayed. In stage three, I also introduce my clients to the concept of signature stories, an extremely useful tool for expressing core values. These are real and tangible illustrations of the core values playing out within the life of your business. Signature stories make it possible for your employees to personally identify with the mission of the company and thereby support uniting your organization under the banner of your core values. Companies that invest in professionally produced signature stories are sure to see impressive returns, both internally and externally.

IMPORTANCE OF CORE VALUE INTEGRATION

Once an organization completes the three stages of core value creation, it is imperative that it continue its work by truly integrating the values into the daily operations of the organization. As a leader, you should always be looking for and seizing opportunities to discuss your core values with your team. Bring them up early and often as part of planning sessions and as part of your monthly or quarterly company reviews.

> AS A LEADER, YOU SHOULD ALWAYS BE LOOKING FOR AND SEIZING OPPORTUNITIES TO DISCUSS YOUR CORE VALUES WITH YOUR TEAM.

Every time I start a quarterly planning session, I have my clients tell me one of their core values and how they are living it out. If your core value is consistency, I want to hear tangible examples from the past ninety days in which employees showed or expressed consistency. I should hear multiple stories and excitement around that core value. If I get crickets, if I hear nothing, then I know there is a problem. Communication is key, and you should be checking in with your team at least quarterly. If you do not do this, you may find yourself in the dark when problems arise. After all, those who don't ask don't know.

Core values should be viewed as tools to inspire organizational behavior that is consistent with the overall mission of the company. Getting this right in a business is the number-one way to build a strong and enduring culture, and it is the foundation upon which healthy enterprises are built. Zappos.com, an online shoe and clothing retailer, is an excellent example of a company that expresses its core values at every level of the organization. Early on, the company's leadership decided to be an organization that delivers great customer service, and they backed it up by identifying core values that align with their purpose. Just run a Google search for "Zappos customer service," and you will find story after story of Zappos employees going above and beyond to deliver superior service.

One story details a customer service call that lasted over ten hours, while another is a heartwarming story of the company sending flowers to a customer who had just lost her mother. One of the more humorous examples of the company's superior service came from Zappos CEO, Tony Hsieh. He shared that one evening, while traveling out of town, he and some vendors returned late to the hotel. Hungry and craving pizza, the group called room service but was disappointed to find that it had just closed for the evening. Hsieh suggested someone from the group call Zappos, and although he may have been joking, the group did exactly that. Once connected, the hungry travelers explained their predicament to the Zappos customer service representative. The rep, unaware of Hsieh's presence, placed the group on a brief hold to gather a list of pizza places that would deliver to the group's hotel. Zappos does not sell pizza but that did not stop this employee from going above and beyond to deliver great service to hungry potential customers. This is an inspiring, real-life example of a Zappos employee living out the company's core value of delivering *wow* through service.

EFI—CORE VALUE DEVELOPMENT EXAMPLE

EFI, an Insight CXO member with eighty-plus employees, developed its core values and action plans in 2015. We began the process in January, and by month five, the results were powerful. However, the process took a twist before they landed on the right core values. During the first four months, the leadership team did a great job of creating core values and detailed descriptions for each one. They even used pictures to provide a visual illustration of each core value. Then, right around month four—roadblock! At the very moment EFI's planning team was supposed to begin implementing the core values, they noticed something was off. The values looked right, but they did not *feel* right. The team was concerned the employees would not embrace the values and might even reject them. Admittedly, the team was a bit discouraged, but rather than giving into the fear, they pressed forward. They examined their wording and, with great focus, worked to identify areas of concern. As a result, the team reworded the values. They did not change the values—just the labels. Here's what they came up with:

- **MAKE A DIFFERENCE**—This is their overarching, one-phrase core value.

- **R**espect Every Individual

- **L**ead with Humility

- **F**ocus on the Improvement Process

- **A**ssure Quality at the Source

- **W**inning Attitude

To help everyone remember, they turned the first letter of the core values into this mnemonic: Real Leaders Find A Way. However, EFI leadership did not stop there. They set out on the next phase of the journey: core value development and implementation throughout the business. There are huge core value banners hanging from the ceiling, RLFAW T-shirts, specific candidate interview questions designed to identify those who align with the organization's values, and even full-company "town hall" meetings that rotate through highlighting each of the company's core values.

EFI's story is a great example, because the process took a twist before it finally landed on the right core values and adopted them company-wide. This is real life, and getting the values right—even if it means delaying full-company adoption—is a move that will pay dividends. EFI dug in, drew on its core, and knocked it out of the park!

STANDING BY YOUR CORE VALUES

A company should be willing to take an economic hit to defend its core value. If not, the core value is not real. In 1982, Johnson & Johnson stood by its core value of "patients first" when it removed every bottle of Tylenol from every store shelf around the world following several deaths due to cyanide poisoning. Even though authorities quickly learned that the introduction of the poison to the pills occurred *after* the bottles left the factory, Johnson & Johnson voluntarily took a multimillion-dollar hit by wiping out their entire inventory. A short time later, they reintroduced Tylenol with the new, tamperproof top that we see today.

Conventional wisdom would indicate that there was no coming back for Tylenol. Regardless of fault, their brand suffered a massive hit. However, within one year of returning to the market, Tylenol surpassed its previously held number-four market position to land in the number-one spot, a position the preeminent pain reliever continues to hold today. The market witnessed the company living out its core values, even accepting an economic hit to do so. Consumers responded en masse to Tylenol's integrity by saying, "That is the kind of company I want to buy stuff from."

SUPPORTING YOUR CORE

As I shared earlier, I learned early on that to reach peak performance on a mountain bike, I had to focus on the strength of my core. As an aspiring pro athlete, I decided the best way to accomplish this was to hire my first strength-training coach. I needed the coach to make sure that I was working as efficiently as possible and focusing on the right things while working within and around a host of constraints. The coach helped me focus my efforts and design a workout plan that maximized every training opportunity.

The strategic workout plan developed by my coach was critical to my racing success. But what if, after investing in the coach's guidance, I decided to ditch the training plan and wing it? Would I have been able to develop the strong core or increased stamina necessary to succeed in racing? Likely not. A plan only realizes its value when it is properly applied, and like my training plan, a business's core purpose and core values are only as valuable as the organization allows them to be. If you don't have a team that is dedicated to supporting and strengthening them, then what is the point? Why have them? If a member of your team neglects those values, goes against your purpose, or otherwise makes it difficult to live by those values, then he or she is of no value to your company, and keeping that employee is likely doing significant damage. But when you build the right team around those values, and each member actively supports that core, then you have the strong foundation needed to achieve your Epic Win.

ENFORCING AND LEVERAGING CORE VALUES FOR AN INTENTIONAL CULTURE

Often, when working with clients I hear questions like, "How can my organization ensure we have the right team in place?" or "How can core values help us create an intentional culture?" I get excited when I hear these questions, because I know the team is ready to apply the concepts. To start, I introduce the senior team to the following categorization matrix. This tool helps define employees by considering how they align with core values and by evaluating their job performance.

As a first step, the senior team needs to create a matrix that ranks all employees in the company (leadership included) as one of the following:

- "A" player

- "B" player

- "High Risk" player

- "C" player

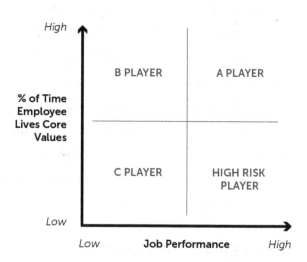

CORE VALUES

The **Y-axis**, or vertical axis, represents core values measured by the percentage of time employees live the company core values. What percentage of the time are they meeting or exceeding core values?

The **X-axis**, or horizontal axis, represents their job performance. What percentage of time are they meeting or exceeding their role requirements, hitting quota, and so on?

HOW TO USE THE MATRIX

With each person plotted, review each person individually and examine where he or she lands on the chart.

- Employees that land in quadrant A are living the core values most of the time and are also meeting or exceeding their job requirements. **The key action here is discussing and making an action plan to keep this person on the team.** "A" players are hard to come by and need to be on a plan for retention.

- Employees that land in quadrant B live the core values most of the time but are falling short in job performance. New employees generally fall into this category. **The key action in this quadrant is to focus on the specific training or adjustment necessary to move the employee into "A" player status.**

- Employees that land in the High Risk quadrant are not living the core values and generally pull the team down. The conflict is that their job performance is good, and sometimes even excellent, or the perception is that their role would be hard to refill. This quadrant is labeled "High Risk," because this is where many senior teams fail to create intentional culture. Due to fears such as losing revenue or possibly a key customer, they fail to do what is right and healthy for the overall organization. Everyone makes this mistake sooner or later, and I have learned this myself—the hard way. I'm always surprised at how well the company moves on after letting a High Risk employee go, primarily because most employees are willing to step up when a toxic coworker is no longer part of the team. **The key actions here are to meet with the employee and attempt to coach their behavior to meet or exceed the core values, making them "A" players, or acting to remove the person in the least disruptive manner possible.**

- For employees that land in quadrant C, it is time to ask the hard questions on why these people are still in their role. If they are in the upper right of quadrant C, there may be hope to adjust their behavior and increase their job performance. However, be careful about spending too much time attempting to improve "C" players at the expense of sufficient focus on the other three quadrants.

In the next chapter, I will introduce our version of a job scorecard, what we call the Role-Alignment Card. On the bottom of the card, there is a place to score employees in relation to how well they are living the core values. The top of the card is where they are scored on job performance. Using these cards prior to charting each person on the matrix will allow you to complete the matrix quickly and efficiently.

EMPLOYMENT BRAND

Companies need to be intentional about creating the right employment brand. Given that there are more opportunities than candidates, people can be exceptionally selective in their job searches. To differentiate yourself from other potential employers, you need to make yourself like a magnet and attract the "A" players. So, what is your employment brand? What is your message that will turn off the potential "B" and "C" players and grab the attention of the "A" players? How does your company stand out? Hiring the right candidates requires the same energy and thought process that you would use to attract a potential client, and to be successful in today's candidate-driven market, your company will need to draw upon its website, marketing materials, and sales process. Companies that attract "A" players approach employment branding with the same level of commitment they express when developing their product brand. Your employment brand is your reputation, and trust me, whether good or bad, word of what type of employer you are gets around.

FISH WHERE THE FISH ARE

Even when operating in a candidate-driven market, there are steps you can take to ensure that your company finds the right talent. If you use a staffing or search firm, providing it with a documented employment brand will boost its results considerably.

When searching for candidates, be sure to use multichannel sourcing. As I like to say, fish where the fish are! Your company should seek to leverage all hiring avenues, including job boards, search firms, and internal employee referrals. Also, many of the most successful staffing managers are constantly networking. They attend industry events and college job fairs. Some reach out to career training organizations and develop relationships with veteran support groups. They dig into every possible source in their quest for the most exceptional candidates.

You never know where your best finds will come from, but by casting multiple lines, you will eventually find sources that produce qualified and varied candidates. If you stumble upon such a honey hole—that is, a fishing hole with a ton of great fish—you should focus your efforts on that source. Attract as many of the "A" players as possible while there, but be prepared to step back and branch out if the fishing dries up.

VIRTUAL BENCH

Often, companies hang on to their "B" and "C" players longer than they should, just to avoid the pain of the recruiting process and the subsequent start-up cycle. Although this avoids the immediate discomfort a change in personnel can sometimes bring, it can cost the company exponentially more in the long run. Forward-thinking companies avoid this by interviewing consistently, even when there isn't an open position, and thereby consistently building a virtual bench of talent. I have even witnessed organizations hire someone they did not have an immediate place for simply because they knew the person was the right fit for their purpose and values. Some organizational positions are harder to fill than others. If you are fortunate enough to come across a good fit for a unique need within your company, do your best to scoop them up! It may require adjusting your time line a bit, and that is OK. The alternative, however, is not. Should you pass on the diamond in the rough, that candidate is free to take his or her talents to your competitor.

Approaching hiring in this way may feel too radical at first, but trust me, it will set you apart from the competition. If you wait to hire until you are in a state of duress, you are far more likely to make a bad hiring decision. However, if you have a virtual bench of talent to pull from, you are free to make decisions that are right for the company and right for your culture.

To download the "Intentional Culture – Core Values™"
worksheet, go to: www.insightcxo.com/tools.
Also see Appendix A.

INTENTIONAL CULTURE – CORE VALUES™

WORKSHEET PURPOSE:
To identify and name the core behaviors that define the culture and character of the business.

WHO Names of real people inside the organization

1.   4.
2.   5.
3.

Hint: High credibility with peers. Most competent in their roles. Would re-hire this type of person. Positive role models.

WHY Significant attributes or characteristics of the people you selected.

1.   4.
2.   5.
3.

Examples: Trustworthy; Work Ethic; Team Player; Caring; Learner: Open minded; Passionate; Problem Solver; Results Driven

CORE VALUE DEFINITION:	Small set of timeless principles. Standards vs. rules.
	Internally focused. Intrinsic value and importance.
	Independent of type of business you are in.
CORE VALUE TEST:	Must exist within at least one person, preferably majority of the company.
	Must be willing to take a financial hit to protect.
	Must be willing to fire a multiple offender.
	Internal or external.
OUR CORE VALUES:	1.
	2.
	3.
	4.
	5.

CHAPTER 3

EPIC WIN—SETTING THE COMPANY VISION

"Success is no accident. It is hard work, perseverance, learning, studying, sacrifice, and most of all, love of what you are doing or learning to do."

—Pelé

The day I declared my intent to race mountain bikes professionally was also the day I willfully chose to disrupt my life. The inspiration came in response to a question posed to the audience at an entrepreneur event I attended in 2010. America's "Dream Coach," Marcia Wieder, was speaking to our group and asked a question that, at first, left me grasping for an answer. "If you did not have a business to run, financial obligations, or family constraints, what would you do with your life? What would you love to say you've done before your time is up?" Marcia asked.

Attendees offered various answers, ranging from traveling to all seven continents to playing golf on the PGA Tour. At first I struggled to respond to Marcia's question. But then, almost out of nowhere, it came to me, and I announced my answer to the group: "I want to be a professional mountain biker and race in the Mountain Bike National Championships." Almost immediately after giving my answer, I began to question myself and my sanity! It seemed impossible. I was a thirty-eight-year-old guy with a business, family, and responsibilities. Racing professionally had not even been on my radar, and although I found the idea exhilarating, in that moment I began to feel overwhelmed. A goal this big would require a radical amount of discipline and commitment. I realized if I was serious about my desire to become a professional athlete, there was no room for self-doubt. I needed to state my goal clearly and go after it, 100%.

> **A GOAL THIS BIG WOULD REQUIRE A RADICAL AMOUNT OF DISCIPLINE AND COMMITMENT. I REALIZED IF I WAS SERIOUS ABOUT MY DESIRE TO BECOME A PROFESSIONAL ATHLETE, THERE WAS NO ROOM FOR SELF-DOUBT.**

Ideally, an Epic Win is one so big that it is impossible to immediately reverse engineer. My Epic Win was more complicated than just turning pro. My Epic Win was to turn pro *and race in the Mountain Bike National Championships*, which proved to be rather instrumental in my journey. The "and race in the Mountain Bike National Championships" clause served as a powerful descriptor, making my goal something I could clearly envision. I could see myself on a mountain in Sun Valley, Idaho, at six thousand feet elevation, racing against the competition. I could visualize Todd Wells, the winner from the year before, wearing the stars and stripes jersey, lined up right in front of me. I could see it all happening. Whenever I had an issue or a problem, or was just getting physically or mentally burned out, having that clear picture of lining up alongside other professional athletes at nationals was the secret sauce that motivated me to push ahead. Having that vivid image of the Epic Win was invaluable. I became emotionally attached to the vision, and it kept me focused on my goal, especially through the most excruciating of times related to potentially life-altering injuries.

A goal of this magnitude required the support of others and, as such, required me to be extremely clear in my objectives. The clarity I possessed for my Epic Win made it possible for others to join in and become part of my team. The same is true of company teams. Do your best to avoid overcomplicated language when defining your Epic Win. It

> **THE CLARITY I POSSESSED FOR MY EPIC WIN MADE IT POSSIBLE FOR OTHERS TO JOIN IN AND BECOME PART OF MY TEAM.**

is important that everyone from the CEO down to the entry-level workers can easily verbalize the Epic Win to customers, prospects, and other employees. The entire organization should have a clear and vivid description with the image and story of what it will be like when the Epic Win comes true. This is where the magic happens, where you start to gain traction and experience the impact of vision clarity. Just as my clear vision of racing at nationals carried me through the best and worst of my journey, a clear vision of your Epic Win is the special push necessary to motivate your team to do what is necessary to get the job done.

When I founded Insight CXO, it was with the intention of helping the leaders of companies with $2 million to $100 million in revenue break through the ceilings of complexity and into an upward spiral of hyper-growth. I wanted to help business leaders define and achieve their Epic Win. It still surprises me how the basic principles that propelled me to racing success apply so directly to the organizations we work with today. While coaching clients, I like to create the Epic Win in draft form as an initial step and then circle back continuously to refine it over a three- to six-month period. Running a full-day session can produce a good result, but the team will inevitably modify the language over time as the real meaning and power of the Epic Win becomes more solidified.

SEAFOODS.COM—EPIC WIN

Seafoods.com began the process of creating an Epic Win that was to be the "largest protein distributor in North America by 2030"— protein, not just seafood. And although they source and ship seafood worldwide, they chose to own the North America market. This gave the team a focal point to shoot for and gave meaning to their annual and quarterly planning process. But Chad Hollingsworth, Seafoods. com's CEO, wanted to refine the Epic Win even further. Chad desired to see the Epic Win truly connect with everyone in the company. He wanted it to be crystal clear so that team members at every level of the company would know what they had to do each day to achieve it. A purpose so defined that even in the absence of any structure, process, or procedures, the Epic Win would steer everyone in the right direction. Working with his senior leadership, Chad and the team changed their Epic Win to "fifty VIPs in fifty states by 2030." This change provided even further clarity within the organization, because the acronym was well established within the culture, and every employee knew how much sales were necessary for a client to be considered a VIP client. Additionally, considering that the economic value of having fifty VIP customers in fifty states translated to well over $100 million in revenue, the benefits of the Epic Win were clear. Creating VIP-level clients is their top focus, and as a result, the Epic Win is now clearly part of their daily DNA.

HOW TO CREATE YOUR EPIC WIN

While your organization is working to define its core purpose and discover its core values, it is important that you start to consider what your Epic Win may be. Setting an aspirational goal is necessary, as it is vitally important that your organization have a meaningful focal point for the team to rally behind. The unique unifying power of an Epic Win is not experienced in ordinary goal-setting. To realize the benefits, you need a larger-than-life goal that just *grabs you*. Your Epic Win should be far enough out there that you do not exactly know how you are going to achieve it. It should be a stretch for you and your team to accomplish and big enough that it cannot be reverse engineered immediately.

In a world full of constraints and setbacks, an Epic Win pushes an organization beyond its comfort zone to someplace grander. Companies that take this step experience near-immediate benefits. Internally, the journey toward an Epic Win promotes out-of-the-box thinking capabilities and helps develop your organization's efficiency muscle, resulting in a unique ability to get more done in less time and with fewer resources. Externally, an Epic Win sets the stage for your organization to break away from the pack and crush the competition. In fact, the journey often reaps as good, if not greater, rewards than the actual win.

Having facilitated hundreds of strategy and planning sessions, I have found that using the ten-year mark as a starting point for achieving an organization's Epic Win seems to make the most sense for companies. A time horizon longer than a decade often seems to yield one or two senior leaders who just can't get on board.

HAVING FACILITATED HUNDREDS OF STRATEGY AND PLANNING SESSIONS, I HAVE FOUND THAT USING THE TEN-YEAR MARK AS A STARTING POINT FOR ACHIEVING AN ORGANIZATION'S EPIC WIN SEEMS TO MAKE THE MOST SENSE FOR COMPANIES.

Vivid imagery and emotional involvement are key elements when determining your Epic Win. I encourage creating a short version of your Epic Win first and then circling back later in the process to create the picture and imagery. When I announced I was turning pro, I put a metaphorical stake in the ground. But what really motivated me to push through was incorporating the vision of racing at nationals, lined up next to Todd Wells in the famous stars and stripes jersey. The clarity of vision proved crucial to the training and the win.

As you and your team meet, consider the following questions to brainstorm possible Epic Wins for your company:

1. What are your company's inherent strengths? What can you potentially become the best in the world at when it comes to producing or providing to your clients?

2. What drives your economic engine? What drives your revenue and profit?

3. What energizes your team? What drives the passion to do the work you do?

Compile a list of responses, narrowing it several times until you land on an agreeable Epic Win statement. Be sure that your Epic Win is measurable, as you will soon begin measuring and tracking how well your company is moving toward the goal. If what you came up with is not clearly measurable, retune in a way that can be measured.

To download the "Epic Win Creator™" worksheet,
go to www.insightcxo.com/tools.
Also see Appendix A.

EPIC WIN CREATOR™

WORKSHEET PURPOSE:

To create a significant 10 year goal for the business that creates clarity on company direction and gets everyone aligned and excited.

Step 1 What are the Inherent Strengths or Core Competencies in the business? What are you best in the world at?

1.   4.

2.   5.

3.

Step 2 What drives your economic engine? What drives your revenue and profit?

1.   4.

2.   5.

3.

Step 3 What does your team get energized about? What drives the passion to do the work you do? What is your Core Purpose?

1.   4.

2.   5.

3.

Step 4 Combine the top statements from each category above and create a short phrase Epic Win.

1.   4.

2.   5.

3.

Hint: Epic Win's can be stated different ways. Most common are Inspirational, Competitive, Humanitarian and Core Purpose

Step 5 Make sure your Epic Win is measurable. How will you keep score along the way? What are the measures, KPI's?.

1.

2.

3.

CHAPTER 4

WINNING TEAMS—CREATING A HEALTHY AND FOCUSED ORGANIZATION

"The way a team plays as a whole determines its success. You may have the greatest bunch of individual stars in the world, but if they don't play together, the club won't be worth a dime."

—Babe Ruth

Traditionally, individual sports have been defined as those where a player competes without a partner, and team sports have been defined as competitions played by a group of people against an opposing group. Mountain bike racing is viewed as the former of the two, much like running, singles tennis, boxing, and so on. Prior to racing professionally, I believed this individual sport definition to be true. But as I began training, I learned how misleading this view can be. As a professional athlete, the people you surround yourself with are critically important to your performance. Without a strong team to support you, it is exponentially more difficult to execute a BreakAway Move and achieve an Epic Win. In the same manner, the people you choose for your company's team often prove to be the difference between having a healthy organization or a failing one. This truth starts with your senior leadership team.

THE PEOPLE YOU SURROUND YOURSELF WITH ARE CRITICALLY IMPORTANT TO YOUR PERFORMANCE. WITHOUT A STRONG TEAM TO SUPPORT YOU, IT IS EXPONENTIALLY MORE DIFFICULT TO EXECUTE A BREAKAWAY MOVE AND ACHIEVE AN EPIC WIN

Early on in my training journey, I met with Chad Andrews, head coach and owner of Total Cyclist. I was attempting to form my racing leadership team, and he came highly recommended. Chad owns five training centers in North Carolina and was well known for having coached many of the top professional road cyclists around the world. However, before me, Chad had never coached an elite-level mountain biker. Given that I was a bit outside of his normal wheelhouse, and considering my very real time constraints around training, I expected him to turn me down immediately. However, after sharing my story with Chad over lunch, he surprised me. Chad not only took me on as a client, he also revealed to me a plan that made training possible despite my very full life. Chad understood that to get the maximum benefit, my training plan had to consider both my work and family life. Because I was unable to build in the recovery time like most pro athletes, I would have to approach training with an efficiency mind-set and integrate it into my whole life plan.

After hearing Chad explain his efficiency approach, I knew instantly that he would be a valuable member of my senior team and an invaluable coach. His insight and radical approach were unlike anything I had heard before. Chad told me point-blank that adding more time to my training schedule would more than likely *hurt* my performance. Beyond that, he instructed me to get more sleep and cut my training hours, which I thought was crazy at the time. But Chad shared, "Considering your already full life, one extra solid hour of sleep at night is worth two hours of training time." Also, he explained that my body could not distinguish between different kinds of stress. He said that regardless of what I was doing, whether working out in the gym or working on a business deal, stress is stress.

Basically, I was experiencing stress throughout my life, and my body could not distinguish the differing sources. This truth shaped my training approach and influenced my mind-set as I prepared to race, and now I think about this statement in my work with my clients. It is essential that those I coach understand the impact of stress in their own lives. Chad also pointed out the need for me to bring other members onto my team, particularly people who could help with specific needs such as strength training and race-day support. I was doubtful at first but trusted his instruction, and not surprisingly, Chad was once again right. Marc Arnone of Prescriptive Fitness taught me how to strengthen my core and handle the load on my legs, and Ryan Kelley became my guru for equipment selection, bike setup, and race-day course strategy. In the end, the assembled team proved invaluable to my racing success.

FOCUS ON TEAM HEALTH

Most rapidly growing companies experience growing pains and various team issues at one point or another. The key to overcoming these challenges is to first address and correct the issues at the senior leadership level. Companies that do not will find that it is especially difficult, if not nearly impossible, to address problems at the middle and lower levels. When working with a senior team to improve organizational health and alignment, I introduce the "Team #1" concept created by Patrick Lencioni, best-selling author and founder of The Table Group.

According to Lencioni, your company's first focus should be on the members of Team #1, which is typically your senior management team. This team's health is paramount to the overall health of the organization. In no way does this imply that nonsenior management team members are somehow less valuable—not at all! This approach merely recognizes an essential truth in leadership; if an organization's leaders are unhealthy, then that environment will eventually seep into every team under their care. Visualize the structural importance of the hub in a bicycle wheel, with all the spokes radiating out from the center. This is the single point of connection for everything. If the hub is structurally unstable, it compromises the performance of the whole wheel. It is critical that your company understand this truth, as your operational success hinges on it. Once Team #1 is healthy, cascading the concept throughout the company and to the front lines is the natural next step.

TEAM #1

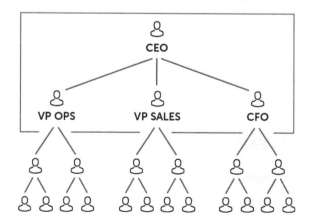

To help illustrate the structure necessary in developing strong teams, I like to use another framework developed by Lencioni in his book *The Five Dysfunctions of a Team*. According to Lencioni, to create a culture of results within a team or an organization, you must first and foremost establish trust. It is imperative that team members trust one another, which means that you and your leadership team need to model this behavior for the entire organization. Employees need to feel safe and trust that there will not be repercussions down the road should they feel the need to offer uncomfortable or negative feedback. Fostering this type of environment encourages getting the big issues on the table so that you can focus on solving problems.

TO CREATE A CULTURE OF RESULTS WITHIN A TEAM OR AN ORGANIZATION, YOU MUST FIRST AND FOREMOST ESTABLISH TRUST.

Organizations consist of people, and where there are people, there is conflict. Some companies may experience this more than others, but sure enough, all will experience conflict. Even so, I often hear team members say, "We all get along, and we have fun together. There is no conflict, so in my opinion, we are very healthy." But truly healthy organizations engage in spirited debates. If your organization seems to never disagree, it is likely your team members do not feel safe enough to voice their opinions. Organizations that suppress conflict are missing out on an important team building and vision shaping dynamic. Some of the best problem solving I have ever witnessed happened deep in the angst of team conflict.

For this reason, I encourage my clients to lean into the hard conversations. However, I also strongly caution them to ensure that teams stay focused on productive dialogue and have zero tolerance for deconstructive conversation or personal attacks. A great way to ensure that your company leverages organizational friction into growth and learning is to make constructive operational analysis inherent within your business operations. Develop a discipline of proactively reviewing team results and performance on both projects and company-wide initiatives, rather than only doing so when something goes wrong. The feedback will begin to reveal successful methods and can even serve as a caution flag, identifying potential problem areas before they reach a critical point.

Open communication and honest dialogue are necessities in any company. However, it is important that teams do not get stuck when addressing a conflict or considering the future direction of the organization. After thoroughly discussing the topic, and once everyone has voiced an opinion, the focus should shift to commitment. This is the point where actual goals are established and plans are developed. Team members must "agree and commit" or "disagree and commit." "Disagree and commit" just means the team member does not agree on the goal or the plan, but he or she is 100 percent on board with the team's decision and will do everything possible to see the plan succeed. Some members of your team may disagree with your BreakAway Move, and that can be okay, so long as those in disagreement wholly agree to support the chosen path as well as the company leadership. Once there is commitment, the team can and should hold one another accountable. When team members feel comfortable enough to exercise accountability, they will reach peak performance and start driving results on a consistent basis.

TANNER PHARMA—TEAM #1

Tanner Pharma Group is one of the fastest-growing pharmaceutical companies in the United States. Headquartered in Charlotte, North Carolina, the company has offices in Europe and clients in more than fifty countries. Tanner is one of the few companies that can claim a core purpose of literally "Improving lives." The company helps people around the world gain access to otherwise-unavailable, specialized pharmaceuticals necessary to their treatment plan. Part of Tanner's BreakAway Move strategy involved merging with a sister company focused on product licensing while also launching a new division in Europe focused on clinical trials. While working with the organization's senior leadership, Banks Bourne, Tanner's founder, asked me, "Robert, what is the most important thing I should be focused on in the next year?" My response was simple. "Banks, you need to focus on creating a Team #1 culture with your senior leadership team."

Soon after my discussion with Banks, the leadership went to work. Once they had their directors in place and pulled all three divisions under one roof, we held an annual planning session and made the "Team #1" concept an annual priority. However, for Tanner to continue its aggressive growth path, the company and its directors had to get this right while also maintaining the culture they had worked so hard to build. This would require radical commitment to the plan. Even with intense global travel, the directors rose to the challenge and scheduled seven multiday, director-only planning sessions in the first twelve months. This was significant, considering each director had his or her own business to run. Leadership spent time learning about one another, discovering their colleagues' strengths, and learning about their fears. The leadership understood the importance of the mission and chose to hedge against potential conflicts by investing in relationships with one another. Their purpose as Team #1 was clear: to help and support one another in leading their respective divisions through future issues and constraints by addressing them in advance. Tanner Pharma's leadership continues to lead their company with an unwavering commitment to the health of the entire organization.

CREATING ROLE CLARITY AND ALIGNMENT

Role clarity and alignment is important to the health of any team. As a first step toward this, I walk my clients through creating Role-Alignment Cards for each role in their business, starting with Team #1. Based on the concept of job scorecards, Role-Alignment Cards have core value behaviors built in and are essentially meant to support alignment and encourage teamwork between the manager and employees.

When creating Role-Alignment Cards, I suggest clients begin with the senior team so that leadership can experience the process and become familiar with how the cards are built. It is important that you work collectively to design the cards, agreeing on the exact look and feel that is right for your business.

KEY ELEMENTS OF A STRONG ROLE-ALIGNMENT CARD

The best way to support role alignment is to be as clear as possible regarding the "what" and "how" of each role in your organization.

THE WHAT

- Title
- Objective
- Relationship to organization's core purpose

- Key accountabilities and functions (prioritizing and assigning the percentage of time each should take)

- Immediate supervisor

- Interfacing departments

After including the basic defining information for each role, it is important that you provide team members with as much clarity as possible regarding what you expect of them. Determine the key accountabilities and functions for each role, prioritizing and assigning time expectations for each. Specify to whom the role reports and list any departments with which the role may commonly interface.

THE HOW

- Role accountabilities

- Role core competencies (aim for 5-7)

- Company's core purpose and core values

- Determining factors for role success

Explaining how you expect team members to execute their duties is as important as defining what is expected of them. If employees hit all their marks but do so in a way that discourages or damages the team around them, you may experience a win in the short run but find the company losing big in the long run. For this reason, I recommend that, in the "how" section of each card, you list the top five to seven core competencies or skills needed for that role. These should be the key attributes the person in the role will need to execute at a peak performance level. Including your organizational core values will help you manage behavior in a way that can be tracked and measured on the Role-Alignment Cards. Lastly, each role responsibility should have measurable and clearly defined corresponding success factors.

IF EMPLOYEES HIT ALL THEIR MARKS BUT DO SO IN A WAY THAT DISCOURAGES OR DAMAGES THE TEAM AROUND THEM, YOU MAY EXPERIENCE A WIN IN THE SHORT RUN BUT FIND THE COMPANY LOSING BIG IN THE LONG RUN.

Although the process of creating Role-Alignment Cards requires organizations to invest additional time, the result is an impressive net positive. Without clearly defined and recorded expectations, how will you know if the person did a great job? Or how might you identify a team member who is falling behind and in need of coaching? Including this information outlines a path to success that benefits both the company and individual team members.

IMPROVE THE QUALITY OF FUTURE HIRES

Once organizations adopt Role-Alignment Cards into their normal business operations, they can draw upon the preexisting information for future recruiting efforts. Each card contains the information necessary to build a comprehensive job description. Consider the efficiency benefits of this, as well as the impact on transparency. Also, using Role-Alignment Cards during the candidate evaluation process allows recruiting managers to clearly rate each candidate based on a full understanding of each role's responsibilities, core competencies, and core values. The increased reliance on data-driven hiring will help your managers identify the best candidates.

In addition to the Role-Alignment Cards, your organization should consider using data-validated behavioral science surveys during the screening process. There are many useful hiring tools that approach hiring from a more scientific perspective. One tool your organization may want to consider using is a behavioral profiles such as the DiSC assessment or the Gallop Strengths Finder. Forward-thinking hiring managers seek to improve their evaluation process by working to gain a deeper understanding of the candidates. I advise clients to consult the tests and surveys as part of an overall strategy to identify the best candidates and steer clear of those who may not be a good fit for the role. However, I caution them to avoid letting tests wholly determine their hiring decisions. Instead, I encourage clients to view personality indicators as part of multistep process that gives more equal consideration to several determining factors. Also, I encourage organizations that use behavioral surveys in their hiring process to continue to leverageand use them as part of an ongoing management strategy. People are unique, and managers that take the time to learn the personality of their direct reports will be able to lead them more effectively and compassionately. Are the employees the type of people who need to hear two nice things before you tell them what the issue is? Or are they just chop-chop, by-the-book individuals? Are there things about their DNA that might trip them up in delivering on their responsibilities? These are important factors, and identifying potential triggers only serves to benefit the entire organization.

> **PEOPLE ARE UNIQUE, AND MANAGERS THAT TAKE THE TIME TO LEARN THE PERSONALITY OF THEIR DIRECT REPORTS WILL BE ABLE TO LEAD THEM MORE EFFECTIVELY AND COMPASSIONATELY.**

Creating and maintaining a healthy team is an essential step in your Epic Win journey. You need the right people on your team, with clear responsibilities, pressing forward to execute your BreakAway Move and achieve the seemingly impossible. To quote Ken Blanchard, a renowned management expert and author of the best-selling book *The One Minute Manager*, "None of us is [sic] as smart as all of us." I would add to Blanchard's quote and say, "None of us are as smart *or effective* as all of us." If you want your organization to break away from the pack and achieve an Epic Win, spend time creating and investing in healthy teams.

To download the "Role Alignment Card Advantage™"
worksheet, go to insightcxo.com/tools.
Also see Appendix A.

THE ROLE ALIGNMENT CARD™

WORKSHEET PURPOSE:
To create a benchmark for each role with vision to the full company goals/objectives and also providing clarity accountability, and success factors. Each person should know how to win.

Title:

Role Objective:

Accountabilities	Priority	% of Time	Success Measures/Goals
*	(1–5)	%	*
*	(1–5)	%	*
*	(1–5)	%	*
*	(1–5)	%	*
*	(1–5)	%	*

Core Competencies and Skills	
1	*
2	*
3	*
4	*
5	*
6	*
7	*

Company Core Values	How the Core Value Relates Specifically to the Role
*	*
*	*
*	*
*	*
*	*

PART II

ACCELERATE GROWTH

CHAPTER 5

THE BREAKAWAY MOVE— SEPARATING FROM THE PACK

"Take calculated risks. That is quite different from being rash."

—George S. Patton

The breakaway move is a crucial element of winning any mountain bike race. It accelerates a race competitor past the race leader and positions him or her ahead of the pack. Timing this move just right is important. Execute it too early in the race, and you increase the likelihood that a fresh rider will be able to match your output, rendering your move pointless. However, if you wait too long to make your move, you risk losing your window of opportunity altogether. And as if timing alone is not complicated enough, it is just one of many strategies competitors need to master to win. As I explained earlier, successful execution of a breakaway move is important, but winning the race requires more. Professional racers spend countless hours in preparation, training and strategizing for each competition. Prior to race day, the most successful competitors will study the course and their competition in detail, often preparing their bikes and pre-riding the race course several times. All of this preparation improves riders' ability to reach peak performance and perfectly time their breakaway move.

BREAKAWAY MOVE

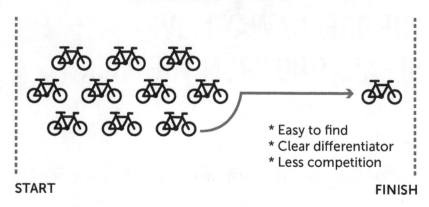

* Easy to find
* Clear differentiator
* Less competition

START   **FINISH**

When a client is ready to execute a BreakAway Move, we begin to focus on identifying potential strategies. When you are ready for the same, you need to determine the best road forward. Be intentional. Work with your team to ensure that your company is ready to perform well enough to stay ahead of pack. To do this, you must stand out from the competition while also continuing to drive revenue and growth. Just as in mountain bike racing, you must be smart with your timing. Executing too early could reveal confidential strategy details to your competition, granting them time to adjust their plans and respond. However, executing too late may result in your message being lost due to a crowded and noisy market. Choosing the correct pace can be the difference between hyper-growth and never edging ahead of the pack.

THE PACK IS NOT SAFE

By all appearances, one would think the safest place in a road bike race would be in the pack. It looks safe to an observer, because we often equate safety with numbers. For a rider, the pack even *feels* safe. Road bike racers experience a false sense of security just by being in the mix. When riding with the pack, riders experience somewhat less wind resistance, and it seems easier to pedal. But the reality is that riding in the pack is far riskier than riding on your own. Pack riding increases your chance of getting caught up in the mistakes of other riders. If one person goes down or bobbles, that rider could potentially take others—even everyone else—with him or her. Pack riding can limit your speed, far overshadowing any advantages gained by avoiding wind resistance. When a racer begins to lose speed, like it or not, it slows down the riders behind them. Additionally, riding in the pack could result in you being stuck at the very moment a breakaway opportunity occurs. Seeing this happen while boxed in, with no ability to respond, is one of the most frustrating feelings in bike racing. The moment you have been training for slips away just five bikes ahead of you while you are stuck in your place. As a serious competitor, your goal should be to be aware of what the pack is doing but to do so from a solitary distance.

The pack misconception is common in business world as well. Many clients seek our coaching because they have been operating with a pack mentality for years. Deceived by the pack's false sense of safety, these companies struggle to gain traction to grow and often feel significant reverberations from the slightest industry market shift. These pack-minded companies also find it challenging to differentiate themselves from their competitors. This is most often because everything looks the same in the pack. Their marketing materials look like everyone else's, and so do their brand promises. They might talk about great customer service, but so does everyone else. Their key differentiators are weak, which makes it difficult for a client or prospect to see a reason to choose their company over the competition.

Be different. Encourage your leaders to avoid the generic nature of the pack. Differentiate yourself early on by creating a clear and compelling marketing position. In business, your BreakAway Move strategy is all about positioning. What are your company's key differentiators? How are your brand's promises unique? What key activities are you doing differently than the rest of the marketplace? Also, be very clear about the functions you are committed to being great at, as well as those you are not. Focus all your energy and efforts into the things that separate you from the pack.

By staying out of the pack, you and your leadership will gain valuable perspective lacking in other organizations. This approach will expose your company to new ways of thinking, ultimately revealing a host of innovative solutions and methodologies that will make you stand out from the crowd.

IN BUSINESS, YOUR BREAKAWAY MOVE STRATEGY IS ALL ABOUT POSITIONING. WHAT ARE YOUR COMPANY'S KEY DIFFERENTIATORS? HOW ARE YOUR BRAND'S PROMISES UNIQUE? WHAT KEY ACTIVITIES ARE YOU DOING DIFFERENTLY THAN THE REST OF THE MARKETPLACE?

DEVELOPING YOUR STRATEGY

In business, developing your BreakAway Move is largely dependent on creating a coherent and simple growth strategy. There are hundreds of different definitions of *strategy* floating around the business world, but the one I choose to share with my clients was developed by Harvard professor and author of *Competitive*

Advantage, Michael Porter. According to Porter's definition, "Strategy is the creation of a unique and valuable position, involving a different set of activities [from competitors]."[1] Essentially, strategy is what your firm does differently to drive new revenue and growth. Your company needs to offer your core customers something that they need and for which they are willing to pay a premium. What does your company do differently from its competitors that results in clients and prospects noticing you? Many companies say they have a unique strategy, but very few do.

MANY COMPANIES SAY THEY HAVE A UNIQUE STRATEGY, BUT VERY FEW DO.

FIVE BREAKAWAY MOVE EXAMPLES

Here are some BreakAway Move examples from major brand companies we are all familiar with. I always find it useful to identify companies who have had exponential growth and look at their BreakAway Moves. Some of these moves are marketing based, and some are more operational. Some are both.

Apple—With the success of the iPod and iPhone, Steve Jobs was still not settled with Apple's growth. He wanted to take his products directly to the consumer and create the Apple Store. Other high-tech product companies tried this before—Gateway, Inc. computers, for example—but Jobs redefined the entire retail experience.

Intel—In the late eighties and early nineties, Intel, like many other chip manufacturers of the time, struggled to scale revenue, because retail demand for their chips was not always there. They were

---

1   Michael E. Porter, *Competitive Advantage: Creating and Sustaining Superior Performance* (Free Press, 1998).

hidden inside a device, and very little attention was given to the value. This all changed when Intel created the "Intel Inside" campaign we are all familiar with today. With this marketing program, Intel was able to educate and influence buyers by making them aware of what they were purchasing. Individuals and businesses who wanted more performance no longer waited for the device manufacturers to create a new class of machine. They would want to buy a machine with the latest and fastest Intel chipset.

Netflix—Netflix has been able to successfully create and execute several BreakAway Moves. Their first move was mailing DVDs to customers versus having them go to a retail location like Blockbuster. The second move was pivoting from DVD distribution to online streaming. Their latest BreakAway Move is the creation of their own award-winning content.

Amazon—Everyone knows Amazon for their online shopping dominance. Several years back, as Amazon was creating a scalable e-commerce infrastructure to facilitate its own growth, they decided to sell their services to other e-commerce–based companies and traditional business as well. Amazon created a high-growth, business-to-business revenue stream from the infrastructure they were already building for themselves.

Ford—Henry Ford, with the vision of producing a car that an average working family could afford, created the assembly line. The success of the assembly line was stunning; however, employee turnover skyrocketed. The narrowly defined and repetitive tasks were burning out employees. In 1914, Ford announced he was cutting back worker hours, going from two to three shifts to create more jobs, and doubling the daily wage. This BreakAway Move reduced annual turnover from 370 percent to 16 percent, and with the productivity boost, the price of the Model T dropped from $800 to $350 over several years. The rest is history.

GETTING THE TEAM ON BOARD

After working tirelessly to determine a new BreakAway Move strategy, leaders often desire to check out a bit and let the process play out on its own. However, I encourage my clients to stay present, because this stage requires strong and focused leadership to ensure that the new plan has full organizational buy-in. The fear of change may cause some team members to resist; however, there are several ways your leadership can manage the process, ensuring that you experience a successful rollout.

First, when implementing a new strategy, be sure to communicate clearly and often with your entire organization. Develop a strong narrative explaining why this is necessary, how the change supports your core vision, and what the impact will likely be for each team. Meet with your senior leadership, working your way down through the reporting structure and ensuring buy-in at each level. Encourage your employees to ask questions, and be sure to answer them authentically. Engage in real dialogue with them. These are the people on the front lines of your organization. Let them know they are a valuable part of your team and that their support is critical to the new strategy's success.

Also, you need to have energy, motivation, and guts to commit to a BreakAway Move and make it stick. It takes extra focus and commitment to do that, but do your best to make sure it is workable all around. You don't want to put your team in a panic by telling them they must work twice as hard to get something done. Instead, work with your senior leadership team to identify opportunities to build excitement surrounding the new strategy. Excitement generates energy, a resource your company will desperately need in surplus throughout this process.

WHAT GOT YOU HERE WON'T GET YOU THERE

An effective strategy should help you fulfill your purpose without violating your organization's core values. It should accelerate you toward your Epic Win and help you double or even triple your revenue in three to five years. The right revenue-driving strategy should be able to accomplish hyper-growth in the right and sustainable way.

Some years back, Marshall Goldsmith, an executive coach, wrote a book titled *What Got You Here Won't Get You There*. Although Goldsmith was applying the logic to executive development, the same is true for your company. The strategy, product line, or service that got your organization to where it is today may not be what gets you to your revenue goal, and it is unlikely to be what gets you to your Epic Win. You need a strategy to fill "the gap."

It is important that your senior team and employees understand the brutal fact that what your company is doing right now may *not* get you where you want and need to go. Most teams innovate or work in the strategy realm just enough to keep up with their industry. If their company is growing at 15 percent, and the industry is growing at the same pace or faster, they think they are okay. However, they are not OK—not in the least.

Great strategies drive revenue and outpace the market. But most companies do not spend enough time on strategy, primarily because they operate by reacting to current industry forces rather than making decisions on what is coming down the road. As a result, they are often fighting to increase revenue. Another common mistake companies make is trying to implement a BreakAway Move without the proper operational system in place. They do not have defined core values or core purpose, and their team is anything but healthy. They have not firmly established annual, quarterly, monthly, and weekly meeting rhythms (which we will discuss further in Part III). Without operational muscle and disciplined teams, they are unable to make their BreakAway Move stick.

NOW IS THE TIME TO FOCUS

Most companies spend their early years focusing on mere survival. This stage fosters a mind-set in founders that is difficult to shake off, especially as circumstances change. However, as your company grows, you need to start thinking ahead and determining where future growth may occur. This is quite the shift from the early days when you were just fighting to get numbers on the books. Furthermore, if what got you here won't get you there, what type of strategy will? How will you implement it and what operational management approach will you employ? Most small to midmarket companies struggle with this and thus make the mistake of equating revenue focus with fear. These organizations find it difficult to make the mental shift from start-up mode, where you take revenue wherever and whenever, to strategic growth mode, where focusing may result in letting go of some things. However, at some point, you must gain focus and break away.

> **AT SOME POINT, YOU MUST GAIN FOCUS AND BREAK AWAY.**

CREATING THE URGENCY

A simple exercise can highlight the importance of having a BreakAway Move to rally behind and drive revenue growth. First, you need to map out the product and service offering for the next three to five years and reveal how close you are to doubling the business. Can your existing products and services, without modification or changes to your overall company, get you to double your current revenue? If yes, congratulations! If no, don't be discouraged. Keep reading and begin to map out how your company can double its revenue. Sustainable growth does not happen overnight; it takes time, commitment, and a plan.

Begin your mapping effort by generating a spreadsheet.

1. In the far-left column, record all your revenue-generating functions.

2. Across the top row, list out years one through five.

3. Fill in the body of the spreadsheet, recording how much revenue each function will produce. Base these figures on current market insights, company structure, and company dynamics.

4. Can you double or triple revenue in three to five years without some intentional changes?

To download the "Define the GAP—5 Year Targets™" worksheet, go to insightcxo.com/tools.
Also see Appendix A.

---

5 YEAR TARGETS – DEFINING THE REVENUE GAP

WORKSHEET PURPOSE:

To determine where the revenue GAPs are based on current offerings or growth strategy.

	Year 1	Year 2	Year 3	Year 4	Year 5
REVENUE TARGET					
List Current Products or Services					
*					
*					
*					
*					
TOTAL CURRENT PRODUCT/ SERVICE REV					
TARGET - CURRENT = THE GAP					
List BreakAway Moves					
*					
*					
*					
*					
TOTAL BREAKAWAY MOVE PROJECTION					

ACTION ITEMS: Top 3 Things to Start Addressing the GAP

1

2

3

CHAPTER 6

BREAKAWAY MOVE DEVELOPMENT—CREATING GAME-CHANGING STRATEGY

"The essence of strategy is choosing what not to do."

—Michael Porter

A BreakAway Move should be focused on driving top-line revenue and not be confused with operational efficiency or execution. Expanding a warehouse, for example, is something that might go in your annual plan as something that facilitates revenue growth but, in and of itself, does not constitute a BreakAway Move. A BreakAway Move should be more top-line and significant. This approach will help keep your team focused on strategy when they may otherwise feel tempted to return to their comfort zones of execution and tactical projects. In most cases, a new capability will need to be developed, or structural company changes may be needed to execute the plan. At this stage it's important to focus on the value of the strategy and not get too wrapped up in the how. The how will be sorted out later.

Getting strategy right is a foundational component of driving top-line growth in business. A well-crafted strategy can help your company drive through the many challenges plaguing businesses today (e.g., real-world constraints, industry and global trends, hiring limitations, and so on). But strategies can be difficult to develop, and there is no single strategy development process that works for every company. Some of our clients can develop an effective strategy simply by focusing on the organization's top priorities, while others need to start with a blank slate. For those that fall in the latter category, I developed a unique process that helps businesses attack strategy from different angles using a mix of tactics and questions from some of today's strategy thought leaders. The BreakAway Move Brainstorming process, outlined below, helps leaders identify the right strategy for their organization.

BREAKAWAY MOVE BRAINSTORMING PROCESS

Part one of the process describes the overall framework we find most conducive in BreakAway Move Brainstorming, and part two contains various exercises that expose the nuts and bolts of generating your list of possibilities.

PART ONE

START SMALL

Generally, the best approach is to work with a smaller, more senior team of seven or fewer people (ideally a group of five). Any more than that and the brainstorming process will most likely get bogged down, and the meeting can lose its momentum quickly.

SET ASIDE DEDICATED TIME

We recommend scheduling half or full-day sessions, off-site if possible, to keep this separate from the whirlwind of daily business operations. If your company does monthly or quarterly planning already, don't try to squeeze brainstorming into a one-hour slot on your agenda. You chance diluting both the planning session and the BreakAway Move session.

CONSIDER USING A FACILITATOR

Our clients tell us that having a facilitator or coach is very helpful. We hear that the facilitator encourages the team to stretch and go deep while also keeping the agenda moving forward and ensuring the conversation stays healthy. When facilitating a BreakAway Move session, Insight CXO team members follow a process we designed specifically for this purpose.

> **THE FACILITATOR ENCOURAGES THE TEAM TO STRETCH AND GO DEEP WHILE ALSO KEEPING THE AGENDA MOVING FORWARD AND ENSURING THE CONVERSATION STAYS HEALTHY.**

PART TWO

SWeaT: THE WARM-UP EXERCISE

Perform the SWeaT exercise as outlined below. The objective of the SWeaT exercise is to promote proper context and global thinking. This gets the team warmed up, out of the weeds, and above the tree line.

- **S** = inherent **Strengths**

- **Wea** = inherent **Weaknesses**

- **T** = existing global **Trends**

1. What are the **inherent strengths** of the company, and what are your core competencies? What has made your company successful over time? These are the things you can leverage to enable your strategy.

2. What are the **inherent weaknesses** of the company that are not likely to change? Most teams struggle with this, as most think all weaknesses can be overcome. Have the team focus and think about the two to three things that the company does not have control over and, as such, cannot be solved within a year or two.

3. What are the **global trends** and economic factors that may affect your customers, your firm, or your people? Have your team members spend at least 50 percent of their time on trends. This is what really gets them above the tree line (strategically) and hopefully identifies things that could really help the company grow—or could potentially create a roadblock if not addressed.

The SWeaT exercise should take sixty to ninety minutes total. Once complete, instruct your team to identify the top two or three items in each category.

MAP OUT THE COMPETITION

Understanding what your organization is up against is vitally important to your BreakAway Move strategy. To help clients better understand this, I guide them through creating a competitive matrix spreadsheet. We do this by creating rows of direct, indirect, and possible competitors, with columns describing things like features, benefits, markets, and capabilities. This can be done on blank paper, whiteboards, sticky notes on a wall, a spreadsheet and projector, and so on.

Let the team really explore what the competition is doing. The more columns you include, the more information you can gather. This will prove useful as your team works to gain insight into your market and understand where the investment capital is going. The spreadsheet may also help you identify your next competitor and what other, related markets your company could enter.

PUTTING IT ALL ON THE TABLE: CREATIVE QUESTIONS

Work with your team to explore the following series of questions and strategy builders. Remember that there are no bad ideas or thoughts at this point. Don't dismiss an idea too quickly. Doing so may discourage others from sharing and thereby diminish creativity and out-of-the-box thinking. Surprisingly, going down the proverbial rabbit hole can be a great method to discover powerful insights into future possibilities. The detour may spawn a new idea that would not have been uncovered otherwise.

A good technique to control the flow is to initiate a *positive* round of discussion followed by a *negative* round of discussion for each idea presented. Using the SWeaT and the competitive matrix as the foundation, ask your team the following questions:

- **Where will the next battle be won? What is the new frontier? Where is the market going next?** A good example of this is Facebook's focus on mobile technology after going public. They decided that mobile was their next battleground and focused heavily, committing time, energy, and money in their mobile strategy development efforts. And as of this writing, Zuckerberg is most excited and focused on virtual reality and in connecting every human on the planet. *Note: Much of the information needed to answer the questions in this bullet point is already contained in your completed SWeaT document.*

- **What has been tried before, either internally or by your competitors, but did not work?** Given the constantly fluctuating markets and the ever-evolving nature of technology, you may have clients and team members who can make something work now that failed in the past. Retrace your company's steps back to the beginning, and take a second look at what did not work. What if you tried the same thing today, with the ability to leverage global platforms like Facebook or LinkedIn, or newly introduced software? Gateway tried opening retail stores without success. Under Steve Jobs, Apple launched the Apple Store, created the Genius Bar, and changed how we think about retail.

- **What two or three existing features, functions, or ideas can you put together to create something unique and valuable?** This could include combining a product and a service. The Hershey Company combined chocolate and peanut butter to create Reese's Peanut Butter Cups. Of all the strategy brainstorming questions, this is my favorite, because it combines two existing, proven things to create something new and unique. There is little risk in merging two proven models, products, or services.

- **Which companies already have a trust relationship with your prospects? When your company does great work for your client, who else wins? What other companies get some type of benefit when you do well?** Many times, your client is required to or already has some other product or service in place before they can buy and use yours. These instances are great business development opportunities. The opportunity to cross-sell products or services and leverage another company's sales force and existing trust relationship with its clients can be a game changer. This was an early BreakAway Move for one of my first companies, AvidXchange.

- **Is there a way to coordinate the uncoordinated? Is there a way to create a platform or exchange-type business that has several core customers? How can you bring clarity to confusion? Is your market fragmented? Are your customers fragmented? How can you connect the unconnected?** Think about what Uber did to connect drivers with passengers and how they essentially have two different customers being served on one platform.

- **What can you own? What can you control?** What kind of roadblock or barrier to entry can you create for your competition? What supplier or vendor relationship can you lock up to create heartburn for your competition?

- **If you were to acquire another company, who would it be, and why?** This is great for teams to discuss. Looking at competitors or similar companies that could extend your offering is a great way to stimulate new thinking within your team.

- **Where are the bottlenecks in your industry? What has been the constant problem that nobody has been able to solve? How can you turn the bottleneck into a strength?** At the turn of the twentieth century, John D. Rockefeller realized that a bottleneck in distributing his refined oil was due in large part to railroad infrastructure and wooden barrels. He began to buy up the rail lines and barrel producers to make sure his product had priority over his competitors'.

- **On what brand promises and differentiating activities can you outperform the competition?** Southwest Airlines has the three "LFs": Low *Fares*, lots of *Fun*, and lots of *Flights*. These three brand promises have been Southwest's core strategy from its early days. Southwest will only go into a new market if it can execute on all three of its promises.

- **If you were to create a new company that was purpose-built to compete with and crush your current company, what would it be, and why?** Assume there are no legacy issues holding you back. This is a great question to uncover blind spots and potentially find new product or service ideas to enhance your current business.

After going through this process, your team should be well informed and aware of the current market in which your company operates. At this point, discussion may begin to develop surrounding a major strategic pivot, such as targeting specific companies for acquisition. These can be major moves, requiring a significant refocus of the company and providing a powerful and strategic path to hypergrowth. The goal is to complete the session having determined two or three BreakAway Moves that the team is energized and excited to work through.

AVIDXCHANGE—ASKING THE RIGHT QUESTION

In 2000, at the age of twenty-nine, I cofounded a company called AvidXchange and served as the VP of Business Development. By 2017, the company had grown to more than 1,000 employees and has recently had two very large financial technology private equity funding rounds in the United States. Bain Capital led at $225 million with a full-company valuation of $600 million in the summer of 2015 and another $300 million round with a full-company valuation of $1.3 billion in the summer of 2017! To date, this has been Bain's largest single investment in any company.

In the beginning, we were referred to as a market maker focusing on the larger commercial property management space. This was just a nice way of saying we had a product that was brand new and a target market that was totally unfamiliar with our "high-tech" solution. I can remember people saying, "What is your company's name again?" and "What do you do?" and "Why do I need this?"

During one of the larger annual commercial real estate trade shows, I was looking for a way to create a path or mechanism for our sales department to improve its performance. Specifically, I wanted to accelerate our ability to have meaningful conversations with prospects and improve our ability to close deals fast, but being a start-up, our sales team was small and already taxed.

While at the show, I asked myself a BreakAway Move Brainstorming question: "Who already has our target customer as a client and has a trust relationship with them?" The answer to this question turned out to be a game changer for us and soon became the early growth strategy that put the AvidXchange on the map. All companies that manage a large amount of commercial real estate have real-estate-specific accounting systems, and there were several well-known industry players with long-standing client relationships at the show. I asked myself, "What if AvidXchange could partner with these accounting firms by integrating our vendor payment solutions into their software?" The approach seemed like a win-win. The accounting firms would benefit from providing their clients with a new feature while likely realizing incremental revenue from their existing client base—a potential BreakAway Move.

The accounting software firms all jumped on board, not only integrating our solution into theirs but also facilitating introductions for us to their existing customer bases. The fact that we were new and had no name recognition did not matter. A trusted relationship started the conversation, transforming our company from "start-up" mode to "scale-up" mode in short order.

TURNING BRAINSTORMS INTO REALITY

Now that your team has generated some strategic, out-of-the-box ideas, it is time to apply them to current customers. To make the BreakAway Move real, you need to do three things:

1. Define who the core customer is or will be.

2. Define the space you want to own, which we will call the "sandbox."

3. Define the unique attributes of your company (its truly unique and hard to copy qualities—for instance, its brand promises).

CREATE YOUR CORE CUSTOMER BUYER PERSONA

Start this practice by examining your current client base to identify the clients you would most like to clone, over and over. Who spends the most money with you? Who understands that sometimes, better things cost more? Who is great to work with and willing to tackle issues together? Who is appreciative and says "please" and "thank you"? Who is willing to refer you to other clients for doing great work?

After creating your list, examine it and attempt to identify any commonalities. What is these buyers' persona? What makes them tick? What are their needs and fears, at a personal and company level? Eventually, you should be able to see the buyer persona take shape and visualize an actual living and breathing person. Pick five of your top clients or target clients, and take note of the person there who ultimately holds the buying authority. Write down all the attributes of the person.

- What is he or she like?

- What kind of car does he or she drive? How does he or she make buying decisions?

- Does he or she use the Internet to research decisions?

- Does the person get his or her information from trade shows or reach out to colleagues for referrals?

- Does he or she decide on things solo, or use groups or teams for final decisions?

At the end of this exercise, pick the top three to five key persona identifiers for your core customer. All aspects of your new strategy will need to resonate with this group and fit into how they operate and buy things.

SEE YOUR CORE CUSTOMERS IN THEIR WORLD

What are the major jobs to be done by your client? Without thinking about your product or service, draw a circle on a blank sheet of paper, write down the ideal core customer that you created earlier, and begin to record all the "jobs to be done," or duties and responsibilities this person holds.

- What is most important?

- What is not being solved?
- Where is there high risk of failure?
- Where is there opportunity to streamline, save money, etc.?

The idea is to get inside the head of your core customer, seeing and experiencing the world from his or her perspective. This methodology served as the foundation for the creation of Insight CXO. We drew a circle around the CEO of a midmarket company and recorded all the things that person was responsible for as CEO. What we saw was a way to bridge strategy with accomplishing goals (a.k.a., execution).

> **WHAT WE SAW WAS A WAY TO BRIDGE STRATEGY WITH ACCOMPLISHING GOALS (A.K.A., EXECUTION).**

WHAT SPACE DOES YOUR COMPANY OWN?

Decide and define the space you want to own in your target market. I call this your sandbox. Imagine a real sandbox, with four walls that hold in the sand and serve to keep damaging influences out. Your sandbox should be just big enough to allow you to double your business in three years and just small enough to still allow for manageable focus.

The BreakAway Move creates a platform for high growth, at least a 33 percent revenue increase each year.

> **YOUR SANDBOX SHOULD BE JUST BIG ENOUGH TO ALLOW YOU TO DOUBLE YOUR BUSINESS IN THREE YEARS AND JUST SMALL ENOUGH TO STILL ALLOW FOR MANAGEABLE FOCUS.**

Use a three-year time line for determining what is inside the walls of your sandbox. Also, think of your sandbox as containing the key market components you want to dominate, essentially the space you want to "own." Once you have these insights in hand, you also have the information to build a brand promise.

DEVELOPING YOUR BRAND PROMISE

With your core customer persona and newly defined sandbox in mind, it's time to start working on your company's key differentiator: your *brand promise*. Done correctly, it can have a powerful impact on how you market and run your business.

Brand promises are custom built to address the needs of your core customer and the area you want to own (your sandbox). A truly effective brand promise answers the following questions:

- What are the products or service areas on which you want to focus?

- How big do you want to become?

- What vertical industries will you focus on?

- Will you use a direct sales force? Internet sales? Independent reps?

- What field can you be number one or number two in?

Think of brand promise as the tip of a large iceberg. Above the waterline is the brand promise: what the world sees, hears, and experiences. This should be what draws prospects to your brand and compels the right ones to buy from you. Below the waterline, where most of the iceberg's mass exists, are all the systems and processes your company has created and developed to execute on your marketing promise.

As you begin to develop your brand promise, think about the "normalized pain" that your core customer persona manages in their position. They are so used to living with certain issues that they are not even aware they have a problem. How valuable might your organization become if you create a solution to a problem they didn't even realize they had? You and your services suddenly become indispensable.

A brand promise is not generally meant for your entire client base; it is meant for the benefit of your core customers (those that operate inside your sandbox). When developing your brand promise, be sure to push through creative dry spells. Keep digging deeper and examining your operations. This behavior makes it hard for competitors to mimic or copy your brand promise. Unfortunately, many companies mistakenly stop the process when creativity and dialogue slows. Do not fall prey to this; push through the drought until the right idea surfaces.

The outline below lists steps useful in creating your brand promise:

1. Create a list of needs—not just wants—for your core customer.

2. Write down your competitors' offerings, focusing on the sandbox area, which is much smaller than the competitive matrix list.

3. What is your company currently "the best in the world at," figuratively speaking? What are its core strengths, or what could be a core strength with some smart operational tuning?

Your brand promise should live in the area outside of what your competition is offering or promising and should coexist with your core customer's needs and your own core strengths.

Once you have created a brand promise or brand promise candidate, run it through a test to see if it qualifies. By definition, your brand promise needs three things:

1.   It should be something your core customer absolutely needs, not just wants. Customers "want" stuff all the time, but you must focus on their core needs.

2.   It should be difficult to accomplish and hard to copy. Your competitors should be scratching their heads, wondering how and why you are doing it.

3.   It must be measurable. You and your clients should be able to measure how well you perform against your brand promise.

BRAND PROMISE

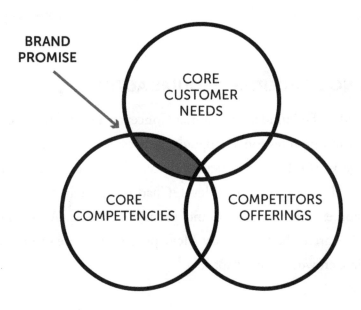

Being able to measure yourself against your brand promise is the Holy Grail of leading a company. It is a great metric for the leadership team, because it is how you know if your operations are really supporting your sales and marketing efforts. But be sure to avoid investing time and resources into a brand promise that nobody cares about. Refine it until it

> **BEING ABLE TO MEASURE YOURSELF AGAINST YOUR BRAND PROMISE IS THE HOLY GRAIL OF LEADING A COMPANY.**

is *just right*. Spend one to three months on generating traction for your brand promise, and then use the world as your lab. Start verbalizing your brand promise with clients and prospects to test their reaction. Start playing around with how the brand promise is represented on printed material, your website, and so on. You are looking for positive reactions from your clients and prospects. The messaging and value proposition should help motivate your core customers into faster and higher-volume buying decisions. With these factors in mind, you can truly begin creating a solid working list of your BreakAway Move candidates.

TRAINING CONCEPTS—REQUIRE ACTION

Chad Todd is the founder of Training Concepts, a company specializing in helping professionals upgrade their careers or increase their knowledge in the IT infrastructure space. He desired to grow his business and take it to the next level. Chad really latched on to the core customer, sandbox, and brand promise concepts. As a result, he quickly started the BreakAway Move process to create something unique in a crowded market space.

Often, when I begin working with new Insight CXO clients, I hear comments such as, "We can't have just one core customer buyer persona," or, "We have too many types of clients." Training Concepts is a perfect example of this. Fifty percent of their revenue is business-to-business. Companies send their employees to Training Concepts to learn the latest and greatest in IT platforms so that they can better run and manage their IT infrastructure. The other half of their revenue is business-to-consumer, where they work with the underemployed and unemployed, typically in partnership with government workforce agencies focused on upgrading employable skills. And although Training Concepts initially thought it would be too difficult to determine just one customer persona, I asked the team to suspend that thinking and work to find the common thread between their business-to-business clients and their business-to-customer clients. To their surprise, they could identify seven attributes that described their core customer.

The process of reviewing Training Concepts' three goals and creating their sandbox ultimately revealed the market space they wanted to own. The company desired to open two new offices in South Carolina and launch a remote learning initiative. So naturally, I asked the team how big their sandbox needed to be to hit their three-year revenue goals. The reality was that with solid execution, they could hit their revenue goals just by focusing their marketing and sales efforts in their home market of Columbia, South Carolina. When thinking about this from an energy, time, and money perspective, the realization proved to be a huge breakthrough!

Next in the process came brand promise creation. Having previously narrowed the sandbox to Columbia, Chad and his team identified a common challenge in their industry. As instructed, the Training Concepts team dug in and created systems and processes (below the waterline, in the iceberg example) and developed a unique brand promise that is hard to replicate (above the water line—the exposed part of the iceberg).

Training Concepts is the creator of the Plus One Promise (+1). It focuses on creating personalized experiences for all its clients, providing the most flexible scheduling options, and making sure each student gets what he or she needs to be successful. It guarantees that its classes will run—a significant problem within the industry—and guarantees that its students will pass their exams.

Where did the "Plus One" name come from? One of the company's core values is "Go Above and Beyond...+1." The way they live their core values is to "Be a +1er." There was so much energy and inspiration around this that they named the brand promise after it. The team gets energized telling prospects about what it means to "Be a +1er" and sharing their brand promise in the form of an engaging story.

In the early years, Chad usually had three or four people on the sales team. But now, with the new marketing message and clarity of focus, the sales team has grown to ten people, with plans to use the new profits to finance expansion into new markets.

Training Concepts' journey illustrates the impact identifying your own brand promise can have on revenue, your team, and your clients.

To download the "SWeaT (Strengths, Weaknesses, and Threats)" worksheet, the "Brand Promise (Define Your Target Audience)" worksheet, and the "Brand Promise (Taking Control of Your Growth)" worksheet, go to insightcxo.com/tools. Also see Appendix A.

SWeaT - STRENGTHS, WEAKNESS AND TRENDS

WORKSHEET PURPOSE:
To get the team above the tree line and in the right mindset for Strategy discussions.

Global Trends
What are the significant trends going on in the world around us? What are the advancements in technology distributions systems, marketing, social media, business models, industry specific changes that could impact the business?

Inherent Strengths/Core Competencies
What are the things that your company has been able to hone over the years and is a source of your success? What do you do better than anyone else? What are you exceptionally good at?

Inherent Weakness
What are the weaknesses or significant constraints that are not easily changed? All weakness can be overcome over time, focus on what can't be easily changed in the next 1–2 years.

Hint: Spend the most time on Trends. Most teams do not spend enough time discussing the world around them

THE CORE CUSTOMER FOCUS™

WORKSHEET PURPOSE:
To define WHO and WHERE the Brand Promise will be created for.

Core Customer
Create a Buyer Persona based on real clients who: Buy for optimal profit, you want more of, say please and thank you, who refer you to others, and see you as a partner.

List names of REAL clients	List the matching key attribute	Short description of your Core Customer
*	*	*
*	*	
*	*	
*	*	
*	*	

Define Your Area of Play—Sandbox
Decide roughly what your 3 year revenue target is going to be. What do you need to dominate to hit your 3 year revenue target? Should be large enough to hit your target and small enough to stay focused. These are demographics, geographics, business lines, channels will you sell through, verticals/horizontals, etc.

List of Attributes	List of Attributes	Short description of your Sandbox
*	*	*
*	*	
*	*	
*	*	
*	*	

BRAND PROMISE—TAKING CONTROL OF YOUR GROWTH

WORKSHEET PURPOSE:

To create a unique Brand Promise that magnetizes your Core Customer to your company and repels the rest. Creates a meaningful platform to tune your operations and differentiate form competition.

BRAND PROMISE REQUIREMENTS:

Must fill a client NEED and not just a want.	Must differentiate you.
Must be hard to do. Hard to replicate by competition.	Must be measurable by you and your clients.
It must encourage your Core Customer to take action sooner.	Typically 1 lead Promise and 2 supporting Promises.

CREATING THE BRAND PROMISE:

Core Competencies	Core Customer Need	Competitors Offerings
*	*	*
*	*	*
*	*	*
*	*	*
*	*	*

Based on the lists above, what are your Core Competencies AND Core Customer Needs that the Competition does not offer? Refer back to the Requirements definition.

CREATING 3 BRAND PROMISE:

Primary/Lead	*
Supporting	*
Supporting	*

CHAPTER 7

SELECTING BREAKAWAY MOVES— PREDICTING THE BEST STRATEGY

"In real life, strategy is actually very straightforward. You pick a general direction and implement like hell."

—Jack Welch

A typical mountain bike race is twenty to thirty miles long and takes one and a half to two hours to complete. Each race consists of three to five laps. Adding to the difficulty, races almost always consist of a tight, single-track trail, making it a challenge to pass other riders. As the oldest pro in the race, I often had to find ways to conserve energy and recover after exceptionally hard efforts. However, I discovered that pre-riding the course allows me identify places to eat, drink, pass, and just rest without worrying about someone coming around me. Also, by being selective about how I manage each course, I can keep my heart rate a few beats lower and thereby control my energy. Trying to pass all over the course and riding on someone's rear wheel are huge wastes of energy and things I avoid entirely. Instead, I am a patient racer. I wait until I reach a designated spot to drop the hammer and always ensure that I have enough reserves in the tank to sustain my breakaway for at least a few minutes. This methodology is the recipe for my BreakAway Move.

> **IF YOU AND YOUR TEAM ARE TRYING TO EXECUTE ON TOO MANY GROWTH INITIATIVES, YOU ARE BASICALLY THE MOUNTAIN BIKER WHO RIDES ERRATICALLY ALL OVER THE COURSE, TRYING TO PASS AT EVERY OPPORTUNITY.**

If you and your team are trying to execute on too many growth initiatives, you are basically the mountain biker who rides erratically all over the course, trying to pass at every opportunity. If you fall into this category, don't panic; this can easily change. Once your team has completed its strategy sessions and created a list of five to ten solid ideas for BreakAway Moves, you are ready to begin the process of narrowing that list down to two or three ideas that your team can really get excited about and support. It is critically important that you use a process to decide which moves to eliminate, as the only thing potentially worse than not having a BreakAway Move in place is for your company to expend precious energy and resources on an initiative that leaves you riding erratically all over the place. Organizational resources are finite, so you must be intentional about every bit you spend.

THE BREAKAWAY MOVE SELECTION PROCESS

I like to organize the BreakAway Move selection criteria into three general categories: energy, time, and cash.

ENERGY

I have assisted countless companies only to find that many seemingly good top-line growth ideas fall flat from the start. The question is, why? Many ideas appear great on paper or on the whiteboard, but once the team starts moving forward, it does not take many speed bumps or roadblocks to stall any of the limited momentum. In most of these cases, if not all, the team was not that excited about the idea and, as such, was not willing to put forward the required effort to navigate through the issues or setbacks. Even if the core values, core purpose, and Epic Win were not mapped out, the team could still sense that the growth idea might be pulling them in the wrong direction; however, there was no process or framework for them to articulate what they were feeling.

Think back to the times when you got a verbal commitment from the team, when in their souls, they were not behind the vision at all. Now think about the projects that you gave little attention to but which the team was behind, in a big way, and they figured things out and followed through to success.

Another factor is whether you have the right people with the right energy. Do you have the right people in place today? Will you need to make any additions to the team to execute? Not having the right people in place is okay only if you have a plan to make the additions quickly. Part of the secret is having the right people with the right energy.

TIME

At the end of the day, the most precious commodity any high-growth company has is time. Time can be thought of in several ways. How much time will it take each week for the leadership team to work on growth, strategy, and execution? Will it take away too much from daily operations? Does the BreakAway Move idea leverage capabilities and processes that already exist inside the company, or will you have to go outside and pull resources in? Will the idea affect revenue this year, or will it take two or three years to generate results? Also, think about the staff in your current structure. How disruptive will the process be? It is always a good idea to go in with some clear expectations on how much time things really take.

> **AT THE END OF THE DAY, THE MOST PRECIOUS COMMODITY ANY HIGH-GROWTH COMPANY HAS IS TIME.**

CASH

Cash is a critical consideration in deciding on a BreakAway Move that cannot be overestimated or underplanned. Some ideas can generate cash as the company grows, fueling growth along the way, and some ideas can suck cash, requiring heavy internal investment or outside loans. Don't be lured into looking just at the high-margin ideas. If the high-margin ideas require additional financing to execute, then at what point could the company run out of cash? This is a simple law of entrepreneurial gravity. Once you run out of cash, the race stops. Some ideas require more up-front, initial investment than others, and some may take longer to generate bottom-line results than others. Are

> **ONCE YOU RUN OUT OF CASH, THE RACE STOPS.**

you and your team willing to take an economic hit this year to set up for a BreakAway Move that could double the business in year two or three? Your team needs to have a discussion and be very clear about how cash, profit margin, financing, and other factors play a significant role in picking the right BreakAway Move.

HOW TO START TO IDENTIFY YOUR BEST BREAKAWAY MOVE

Make a list of all the BreakAway Move contenders on a spreadsheet or, if in front of the team, on a whiteboard. Then create columns from each of the following section headings, and rate each idea on a scale of one to ten, based on team consensus. I have found that having the team discuss the nuances between what is rated a six versus what is rated a seven is helpful.

EXCITEMENT AND ENERGY

In facilitating hundreds of strategy and planning sessions, I've experienced firsthand the power of excitement. Some things are just more fun and meaningful for the company to rally behind. Entrepreneurs have a habit of coming up with great ideas and forcing them through the company, only to get frustrated and angry later when things don't work out as they originally envisioned. The team may get much more excited about opening a new office in a hot market than adding a bolt-on service to the existing business. Often, I find that an idea with excitement and energy behind it gets the focus and attention of the team, and as a result, they find ways to make it work rather than letting things trail off. The team needs to believe there is a big personal and professional win for executing the BreakAway Move. Score a ten if this has a high impact on excitement and a one if it has a low impact on excitement.

REVENUE IMPACT

To qualify as a BreakAway Move, the idea must have the ability to, at minimum, double revenue in three to five years. This does not always have to be the full company's revenue, but to be impactful, it should at least have that impact on a division of the business. A BreakAway Move can involve many aspects of the business, but for our current purpose, focus on its ability to really drive top-line growth. Score a ten if the idea has a high, positive impact on revenue and a one if it has a low impact on revenue.

CORE IDEOLOGY IMPACT

Does the idea get the company closer to fulfilling its Epic Win and accelerating the core purpose? Does it violate any of the core values? This is a critical scoring step. Many times, great ideas don't work because there are knowingly or unknowingly core ideology violations. BreakAway Moves require focus and serious commitment to execute. If there is a core ideology violation from the start, often with money or profit as the root cause, projects will die a slow death. Get this right, and your team will have an energy source to tap into when times get rough. Score a ten if this idea has a high impact on core ideologies and a one if it has a low impact on core ideologies.

> **MANY TIMES, GREAT IDEAS DON'T WORK BECAUSE THERE ARE KNOWN OR UNKNOWN CORE IDEOLOGY VIOLATIONS.**

LENGTH OF TIME

How much time will it take to execute the idea? Are there supportive resources in place today? How much management time will it require, and will it possibly cause issues with the current book of business? As a rule, teams typically overestimate what they can accomplish in a quarter or year and underestimate what they can accomplish in three years. Time is the most valuable commodity in a high-growth business. Score a ten if this idea requires a small amount of time to execute and a one if it requires a lot of time to execute.

CAPABILITIES

If you are lucky, you can pull off your move using your existing people, systems, processes, and core capabilities. But the winning move might require some outside help. A low score in this column is not necessarily a bad thing; it may be the best way to get the company into hyper-growth. But it is important that you are clear regarding what you presently possess and what you still need to develop. This is also a good time to discuss who (outside of the company) could accelerate closing the gap between where you are and where you need to be, capability-wise. This could be an advisor, coach, or consultant. Score a ten if this idea only requires the assets you already have in place and a one if you must develop or buy the capabilities.

PRODUCE OR SUCK CASH

Will the idea fund itself and produce cash as revenue grows, or will it require cash as revenue grows? If it requires cash, are there resources in place to fund it? There is a movement toward creating business models that are funded by customers rather than outside financing. Even the great venture capital (VC) firms openly admit that the VC route is not as attractive as it once was. Private equity is an option, but if you can tweak your model to produce cash and rely less on outside financing, that

> **IF YOU CAN TWEAK YOUR MODEL TO PRODUCE CASH AND RELY LESS ON OUTSIDE FINANCING, THAT IS ALMOST A BREAKAWAY MOVE IN AND OF ITSELF.**

is almost a BreakAway Move in and of itself. Not having to add board members or create unnecessary debt is a good plan. And if your team has a high score everywhere else and a low score here, ask your team what could be done to shorten sales cycles or change the rules so that cash becomes available sooner rather than later. It is often better to pursue the lower profit margin in favor of creating more cash to fund growth. Score an idea a ten if it has a high, positive impact on generating cash and a one if it has a low impact on generating cash or requires cash or outside financing to execute.

PROFITABILITY

One way to increase cash flow is to increase profitability. How much gross profit or net income will the move produce? This will require some thoughtful discussion and possibly some quick spreadsheet work to estimate. A wise person once said, "Revenue is vanity, and profit is sanity!" Score a ten if this idea has a high, positive impact on profit and a one if it has a low impact on profit.

> **A WISE PERSON ONCE SAID, "REVENUE IS VANITY, AND PROFIT IS SANITY!"**

INVESTMENT REQUIREMENT

Does the idea require a substantial investment? Can a small amount be invested to test the idea, or will it require a large up-front check to get it started? Can the investment be made as milestones are achieved? If you believe that this idea will double revenue, how might it affect expenses? Score a ten if this idea requires a low overall initial investment and a one if it requires a high overall initial investment.

NARROWING IT DOWN

Next, have the team discuss, debate, and attempt to reach a consensus regarding how each contender rates in the columns on a scale of one to ten. Use this measurement to narrow your BreakAway Move options down to your top three. The ideas with the highest scores are the best ideas. The only other rules in selecting your final BreakAway Moves are as follows:

1. They should never violate a core value or purpose but should instead support them.

2. They should accelerate your company's progress toward your Epic Win.

3. They should be realistic to accomplish and should be something the team can visualize doing.

4. They should apply directly to all the values and highlighted needs of your core customer or desired core customer.

INTEGRA—A GREAT BREAKAWAY MOVE

At any given time in Charlotte, North Carolina, there are more than two hundred staffing and search firms ranging in size from start-ups to massive, multibillion-dollar global players. Although many claim to have proprietary tools and processes to find the "right fit," most firms essentially offer the same kind of service and generally draw from the same candidate pool. This is what the market looked like in 2003 when I launched Integra Staffing & Search. We were a start-up in a highly competitive space within a $1.5 billion market in the United States alone. Given that most staffing industry players are structurally similar, it was very difficult for hiring managers to differentiate us from the crowd and especially hard for our sales team to break through all the noise in the market.

I grew increasingly tired of the monotony and clone-like behavior in the staffing industry market. To make our company stand out, I introduced the concept of brand promise and brand promise guarantee to the team. They were immediately excited at the possibility we might somehow be able to offer something different, something unique. Immediately, we began developing ideas that would be meaningful to our core customer. "Right fit," "speed," and "best service" were candidates, but they were overused by our competition, rendering them unusable for us. As we dove deeper into the persona of our core customer, we identified that the clients who appreciated us the most were those to whom we could send three excellent, hard-to-choose-from candidates. We decided that if we could focus on securing more clients like this while also identifying a way to replicate this experience over and over, it would be a game changer.

With our brand promise outlined, it was time to give it a name. After several naming sessions and subsequent testing with our clients, we landed on the 3:1 Guarantee™. We guaranteed that if you hired us, and we took you through our hiring process, we could deliver three candidates so strong that you would find it difficult to choose just one. Once we determined the brand promise, we created a logo to represent it and registered a trademark to protect our intellectual property. The results were more staggering than even I could have imagined. Not only was the 3:1 Guarantee the rocket launcher that propelled us to multiple Inc. 5000, Charlotte Business Journal Fast 50, and Best Places to Work wins, it was also the defining factor in determining how we ran the business. The 3:1 Guarantee let the market know how we were different and, moving forward, set a metric by which we could manage our sales and recruiting teams.

The typical staffing firm process can be time consuming and highly inefficient. When attempting to fill a position, prospects or clients reach out to several agencies and ask for résumés. Each agency then attempts to submit as many qualifying résumés as quickly as possible. The client hiring manager is then tasked with sorting through and interviewing twenty-five candidates. I realize this sounds crazy, but this is how the process works. The inefficiency provided an opportunity for us to be different and better. To set our business apart, our sales team would tell prospects that to get our 3:1 Guarantee, they would have to use our firm exclusively, or at least give us an opportunity to deliver ahead of our competitors. However, in the staffing industry, securing clients is only half the battle. To fully deliver on our brand promise, we had to match available positions with the right people. On the recruiting side, our team knew that to have any chance of offering our clients three qualified candidates, job orders and position descriptions had to be exactly right. The big leverage point was using our brand promise to change the way our clients used staffing services in favor of us. We brought added value to the client and increased our business. We changed the rules.

> **NOT ONLY WAS THE 3:1 GUARANTEE THE ROCKET LAUNCHER THAT PROPELLED US TO MULTIPLE INC. 5000, CHARLOTTE BUSINESS JOURNAL FAST 50, AND BEST PLACES TO WORK WINS, IT WAS ALSO THE DEFINING FACTOR IN DETERMINING HOW WE RAN THE BUSINESS.**

PREPARING FOR ACTION

In most companies, the senior team is occupied with a thousand responsibilities throughout the year, and it can be difficult to think about a BreakAway Move when you are occupied with the day-to-day grind. It is important that you work intentionally to avoid stagnation. To ensure that your moves are at the forefront of the team's thoughts and actions, include them in your everyday routine! Put the BreakAway Moves on company and team calendars. Include time to discuss them in your meeting agendas. Bring the topic up on conference calls. Check in with your team to see if they are thinking about the moves. Create a list of the capabilities that will be required to complete your BreakAway Move, and assign those needs to the best people. If you don't have everything you need in-house, start looking outside your normal circles, such as at trade shows and among outside experts. Stay alert, and keep the conversation moving, or else the BreakAway Moves may never happen.

A great technique to add some extra energy behind your BreakAway Move is to give it a name. This way, the team can refer to the initiative in a consistent manner. Also, giving a BreakAway Move a name is like giving it a life of its own. It makes the move seem more obtainable and real.

> **GIVING A BREAKAWAY MOVE A NAME IS LIKE GIVING IT A LIFE OF ITS OWN. IT MAKES THE MOVE SEEM MORE OBTAINABLE AND REAL.**

It takes thought, time, and commitment to simply create a BreakAway Move, let alone implement one. Once it is in motion, it might need to be adjusted as you learn and adapt. Remember that in a race, the first big effort or BreakAway

Move *almost never sticks*. An effective BreakAway Move requires patience and perseverance. After you do it three or four times, you will figure it out. And, once you do, you will have the secret sauce that will allow you to make it stick.

ASSIGN OWNERSHIP AND LEVERAGE SUPPORT

Big initiatives often stall simply because team members are unsure what they should and should not be doing. You can avoid this by assigning BreakAway Move ownership to one person and holding him or her accountable for its progress. Having one person championing the initiative ultimately reduces confusion and streamlines the implementation process. Also, be sure to leverage outside resources to accelerate the execution of your BreakAway Move. Founders are generally not accustomed to asking for help or investing in outside resources to get stuff done, but sometimes it is necessary. Often, successful BreakAway Moves require capabilities that you do not currently have in-house. Considering the potential payoff, this may be the time to consider hiring a business coach, consultant, board advisor, or industry expert.

HOW MANY MOVES AT ONCE?

The number of BreakAway Moves your company can and should handle is largely dependent upon the stage, size, and scale of your business. As a rule, I advise clients to focus on just one to three BreakAway Moves at any given time. Additionally, one of the three moves should receive more attention than the others. This move should take priority and be kept alive even when the daily or weekly whirlwind becomes intense. However, it is good practice to have one or two more moves in the works, as it helps keep the team strategically focused above the tree line, analyzing and questioning where the new revenue will come from.

THE BREAKAWAY MOVE EVALUATOR

Workout Purpose: List your top BreakAway Move ideas and identify the best option through a quantitative scoring process.

BreakAway Move Requirement: To qualify, the idea must have the potential to have a significant impact on revenue in one to three years.

DOES THE BREAKAWAY MOVE...			IDEA A	IDEA B	IDEA C
Growth	Meet or exceed revenue targets?	10 high – 1 low			
Energy	Support the Core Values?	10 high – 1 low			
	Support the Core Purpose?	10 high – 1 low			
	Accelerate the Epic Win?	10 high – 1 low			
Time	How much exec team time	10 high – 1 low			
	How much company time	10 high – 1 low			
	Require capability currently in place?	10 high – 1 low			
Money	Size of initial investment	10 high – 1 low			
	Create cash during growth?	10 high – 1 low			
	Affect profitability?	10 high – 1 low			
	Total score				
	Highest score wins!				

HINT: Have a healthy debate with your team. The exercise's real value is found in how each attribute is ranked. The winner will become clear even without the scoring!

PART III

CRUSH THE COMPETITION

CHAPTER 8

EXECUTION—CREATING A GROWTH FRAMEWORK

"Strategy without tactics is the slowest route to victory.
Tactics without strategy is the noise before defeat."

—Sun Tzu

There are three major elements to successful BreakAway Moves. Part I is having a strong core and foundation to build on; Part II is creating and selecting the BreakAway Move itself; and Part III is making it stick, accelerating past the competition, and holding the lead for the Epic Win.

As I shared earlier, winners in business and racing are not always the strongest or the biggest; however, they are almost always the best prepared. They visualize and plan the race in advance and then control their pace through an efficient use of energy. The winners are wise stewards of their resources. They spend time planning how they will handle the gnarly hill climbs or tight and twisty sections that, in the end, win the race. To execute the Epic Win, you need to have the power and the tenacity to keep accelerating after you pass the competition. After all, what good is a BreakAway Move if you cannot make it stick?

PRE-RIDING: PREPARING FOR THE RACE

As we discussed briefly in Chapter 7, one game-changing advantage I discovered as a pro racer was the benefit of pre-riding a race course. Doing this—often days or weeks before the actual race—gave me an advantage come race day. I spent time figuring out the starting line setup and discovering hidden turns. I would determine where the drop-off was around a blind turn. I took time to survey the big hills and figure out how steep they were. Often I would pre-ride the course the day before the race, but sometimes I had to do it weeks before. This type of planning was critical for pacing and energy management and would have been impossible to do by simply looking at the course map. I could think ahead, visualize what was coming, and make strategy decisions with confidence. Knowing the course up close and personal allowed me to adjust during the race and avoid getting stressed out. And trust me: these adjustments happened in every race. The process of visualizing, planning, and adjusting was how I could control myself and successfully compete with men around half my age. This was my competitive advantage.

> **THE PROCESS OF VISUALIZING, PLANNING, AND ADJUSTING WAS HOW I COULD CONTROL MYSELF AND SUCCESSFULLY COMPETE WITH MEN AROUND HALF MY AGE. THIS WAS MY COMPETITIVE ADVANTAGE.**

CREATING YOUR BREAKAWAY MOVE
EXECUTION PLAN: THE 13-WEEK SPRINT

When applying the BreakAway Move execution plan in business, I consider the racecourse to be based on ninety-day quarters, or what I call 13-Week Sprints. This means planning and pre-riding your "racecourse" in the ninety days, or thirteen weeks, leading up to your BreakAway Move. I often tell my clients, "You really only have control over two things: your Epic Win and your 13-Week Sprint. Epic Wins, with a ten to twenty-year horizon, are only achieved through well-planned, long-term strategy. It is what you and your team do on a daily and weekly basis that converts that strategy into action. Taking the time to visualize and plan your 13-Week Sprints ahead of execution will ensure that the actions you take are more effective, more efficient, and smarter."

Hyper-growth companies are usually run by their founders, who started the companies based on personal experience or knowledge of a specific industry. Most are visionaries and rainmakers. Managing the day-to-day activities is normally not part of their core skill set and is not what gives them energy. They tend to struggle with keeping track of the activities that grow the company. Without an intentional plan in place to push growth initiatives along,

> I CONSIDER THE RACECOURSE TO BE BASED ON NINETY-DAY QUARTERS, OR WHAT I CALL 13-WEEK SPRINTS. THIS MEANS PLANNING AND PRE-RIDING YOUR "RACECOURSE" IN THE NINETY DAYS, OR THIRTEEN WEEKS, LEADING UP TO YOUR BREAKAWAY MOVE.

founders often get caught up in the daily whirlwind of running the company.

The 13-Week Sprint is structured in a way that helps push the BreakAway Move along amid the everyday grind of your company. Each quarter, create a very simple visual display of the company's overall "rocks," "priorities," and BreakAway Move action items, including all the major tasks and milestones associated with them. What is the difference between a priority and a rock? A priority is a significant initiative that is tied to the annual plan and usually takes longer than one quarter to accomplish, whereas rocks are smaller initiatives that can be accomplished in thirteen weeks or less. Given the hectic pace at which most companies operate, it is helpful to have a clear and concise naming practice in place. For instance, when team members use the term "priority," you know they are referring to an initiative requiring a one-year time line. Conversely, if they say "rock," you know they are referring to a quarterly initiative.

Once your rocks are set, it is time for you and the team to move on to completing the 13-Week Sprint tool. This is a major component of ensuring that the quarterly planning process is impactful. During the session, you create your quarterly plan, and before you finish, you break it down into thirteen-week segments.

As part of my Insight CXO coaching program, I have my clients complete a very detailed 13-Week Sprint that has no more than three to five full-company rocks. The rocks must be cross-functional (meaning they involve more than one department) and include at least one priority that drives the BreakAway Move forward. In other words, the 13-Week Sprint tool ensures that the company stays on pace to execute its quarterly, annual, and most importantly its BreakAway Move plan and goals. The tool will also serve as a mechanism to drive accountability and results. Each rock and each line-item task has an owner, someone who is accountable for making sure that task gets done.

The 13-Week Sprint document will guide the team throughout the quarter. They will live in it; it will serve as their home base. Follow these steps, complete each task one by one, and watch your company begin to separate from the pack!

PLAN FOR ADJUSTMENTS

What does your next 13-Week Sprint look like? Can you anticipate what might be in the middle of a blind turn? Have you mapped out your passing zones and determined where you can push and where you might need to hold back? Great companies plan. They take time to pre-ride the next thirteen weeks so that they can identify potential issues and complications in advance. However, even with pre-riding, plans will almost certainly require in-the-moment adjustments. I will say it again; your plans will almost certainly require in-the-moment adjustments. In the life of a hyper-growth company, things often happen so quickly in a quarter that the team must provide constant feedback to ensure they stay focused on the right things. For example, as we start working on rock number two, we should ask ourselves what we have learned since we started the quarter. Is there a way to complete this initiative faster? How can the team improve on the task list? Is there new information available that could make this initiative

----

GREAT COMPANIES PLAN. THEY TAKE TIME TO PRE-RIDE THE NEXT THIRTEEN WEEKS SO THAT THEY CAN IDENTIFY POTENTIAL ISSUES AND COMPLICATIONS IN ADVANCE.

----

more impactful? Great companies ask hard questions and leverage their learning.

As a racer, I entered every one-month training block with a plan. I knew what skills I would be focusing on and how much time I planned to dedicate toward training. However, no matter how much time I spent planning, at one time or another I would inevitably have to adjust. This is true in business as well. A team that can adapt quickly to changing plans is much more likely to outperform their competition.

But being able to adapt is only half the battle. You must also be able to gauge when to make an adjustment and when not to. This is a crucial element, and for me, this was when the role of my coach, Chad, became vital. There were times during training when he would say to me, "Robert, you just have to find a way to make this happen. This is a key workout." Or, more often, he would say, "Robert, skip this workout, and don't try to make it up. You really turned yourself inside out in Sunday's race, and you need the recovery time." Often, work or family would cause me to miss a key workout. When this occurred, I would fear falling behind my competitors, and as such, my instinct was to immediately make up the important training session. But Chad knew this about me. He would reassuringly remind me to stick to our plan, pointing out that my efforts to fit something in may mess up the rest of my training week. Chad's voice of reason was an essential piece of my training and subsequent success. For this very reason, all top athletes and CEOs have a coach; coaches save them from themselves. Managing those adjustments became a key part of my training plan, and Chad's guidance served as an independent and wise voice of reason.

Building a winning 13-Week Sprint plan is easy when you know what to do and accept that any plan is going to need some race-day adjustments.

BUILDING YOUR 13-WEEK SPRINT

Step 1: List Your Rocks

When planning your company's next thirteen-week interval, the first step is to take the priorities that were created at the previous annual, quarterly, or BreakAway Move planning session and list them in the same order on the 13-Week Sprint sheet. As a reminder, best practice is to have no more than five. If you are already performing detailed annual and quarterly planning, make sure at least one quarterly rock is dedicated to a BreakAway Move. Remember, rocks are initiatives that can be accomplished in less than thirteen weeks. This ensures that your longer-term strategic initiatives are getting attention and not being put on the back burner, as happens with most companies. It takes discipline and commitment to do this, but it will pay huge dividends in the long run.

Step 2: Make the Rocks SMART

Next, make sure to review the descriptions of the priorities and verify that they are SMART: **S**imple, **M**easurable, **A**ttainable, **R**ealistic, and **T**ime-bound. The clearer the priorities are, the easier it will be to build the plans around them.

Also, do your best to make the rocks cross-functional; involving more than one department builds teamwork. When a company exceeds fifty people, getting the department heads to work together becomes paramount. Prioritizing this cross-functional approach may be one of the best mechanisms I know for getting people to work, plan, and execute together for the full quarter. BreakAway Moves are almost always cross-functional. With this approach, you create a growth strategy while also strengthening your team through collaborative work.

BREAKAWAY MOVES ARE ALMOST ALWAYS CROSS-FUNCTIONAL.

Step 3: Make Someone Accountable

Assign one person the accountability for keeping each rock alive during the quarter. I like to ask for volunteers for this, but you don't want the same person accountable for all the rocks. Depending on the size of your team, do your best to ensure that the accountabilities are balanced throughout the team. However, the person accountable is not responsible for performing all the work. His or her responsibility is to ensure that the necessary meetings are occurring and that progress is being made. A rock does not have a voice to be heard or a hand to be raised in a meeting to warn others that the team is falling behind, but team members do. Holding one person accountable for keeping a rock alive helps ensure that someone is constantly monitoring progress and raising the alarm should things begin to derail.

Step 4: Create Teams

Have the group create rock teams, with each rock having a cross-functional team assigned to it. Ideally, each rock team should have three to five members. Any less than three and you risk losing cross-functional team building. However, any more than five and it becomes difficult to make progress, as getting everyone's schedule synchronized becomes a large task in and of itself.

Step 5: Deep-Dive Tasks

Have the teams hold a thirty-minute breakout session to deep-dive the rocks and come up with all the small and large tasks that must be accomplished in the quarter to achieve that SMART rock. For example, if it is a rock associated with driving sales, one task may read, "We need to hire, onboard, and train a VP of sales and three sales team members by the beginning of the first quarter." There may be five to fifteen different tasks associated with that one rock.

Step 6: Create Start and Finish Dates for Each Task

Instruct the teams to determine when a task must start and when it must be completed. If you have five to fifteen tasks underneath a rock, each of those tasks should have a start and finish week. Some tasks can be started and completed in one week, and that's great. However, a lot of tasks require more time, even several weeks. It is extremely important that you allot ample time to each task, especially when it requires multiple people to execute.

Can you imagine the chaos that would occur if a mountain bike race did not have a designated start time or starting line? What if the race promoter just said, "This is a three- or four-lap race, the start line is somewhere around here, and the finish line is somewhere around there … Go!" Positioning yourself correctly from the start is mission-critical, whether on a racecourse or in your business.

Step 7: Share the Rock Tasks and Time Lines with the Group

Once you have completed all the necessary information for your rocks on your 13-Week Sprint sheet, including associated tasks and respective time frames, have each team share their details with the entire group. Request that they verbalize their reasoning, step-by-step. What associated tasks did the team identify? Why are the tasks necessary? Ask them to walk through the time frame they identified and explain how they arrived at this specific conclusion. The group should determine whether the tasks are correct and should explore whether there is something another team could offer to help drive the work in question. Do this for each rock, performing adjustments as you go. Given that the full team will have vetted one another's tasks and confirmed the set time frame, this part of the exercise will serve as a major mechanism in driving a culture of teamwork and accountability. With the entire group providing input and offering feedback, they will have a vested interest in seeing their peers succeed.

Step 8: Pre-ride the Quarter

The last step, pre-riding the thirteen weeks, is also one of my favorites. Review all the rocks and tasks collectively, preferably on a large screen or display so that everyone can view it simultaneously. Closely examine how the rocks are stacked on top of one another with their respective tasks. Instruct the team to once again review all the rocks and tasks and attempt to identify any inconsistencies or potential issues. Is there anything listed that might not work? For example, are there too many deadlines on one Friday? Is there an overabundance of tasks concentrated in the first four weeks? You may want to confirm that the time frames take holidays into consideration, and so on. At this critical juncture, the input of the group is vitally important.

A full group review leverages the team's years of business perspective and experience, thereby increasing your chances of identifying potential weak points in the plan. Instruct the team to carefully review the distribution of tasks in your 13-Week Sprint. Are the tasks scheduled at a workable pace? Teams tend to overschedule and put all the tasks into the first month. This is a mistake in most, if not all, cases. Generally, the rocks are initiatives that support your efforts to develop the business and are not part of the normal, day-to-day routine. Realistically, each person has only about one to four hours per week that he or she can dedicate to working on rocks; this is why there is a max of five rocks per quarter and why the team sizes are smaller. Scheduling most of your tasks in the first month would not allow your team the time necessary to perform their everyday duties. Attempting to operate at an unrealistic pace is not healthy for you or your team. Pace the tasks, and pace yourself. Trust me; you will accomplish more in the end.

ATTEMPTING TO OPERATE AT AN UNREALISTIC PACE IS NOT HEALTHY FOR YOU OR YOUR TEAM.

13 WEEK SPRINTS

ROCK #1 DESCRIPTION	OWNER	STATUS	1	2	3	4	5	6	7	8	9	10	11	12	13
Key Task		G/Y/R	■	■	■										
Key Task		G/Y/R		■											
Key Task		G/Y/R					■	■							
Key Task		G/Y/R							■	■	■	■	■		
Key Task		G/Y/R													

ROCK #2 DESCRIPTION	OWNER	STATUS	1	2	3	4	5	6	7	8	9	10	11	12	13
Key Task		G/Y/R	■												
Key Task		G/Y/R			■	■	■								
Key Task		G/Y/R			■										
Key Task		G/Y/R										■	■		
Key Task		G/Y/R													

ROCK #3 DESCRIPTION	OWNER	STATUS	1	2	3	4	5	6	7	8	9	10	11	12	13
Key Task		G/Y/R	■												
Key Task		G/Y/R	■	■											
Key Task		G/Y/R					■								
Key Task		G/Y/R							■	■	■				
Key Task		G/Y/R							■	■					

KEEPING THE 13-WEEK SPRINT ON TRACK

Green—Yellow—Red—Purple

The success of your 13-Week Sprint will largely depend on your team's ability to keep the ball moving forward. But how do you do that, now that you have built your plan? How does your team keep the 13-Week Sprint moving forward? The best way to avoid having your plans fall by the wayside is to review your progress during weekly or biweekly meetings. Each rock and each task has an owner responsible for updating the status *before* the weekly or biweekly meeting. To ensure that updates are simple and clear, I designed a color-coded system that indicates the task's status.

- GREEN = Tracking as planned

- YELLOW = One week behind

- RED = Two weeks behind

- PURPLE = Complete

- NO COLOR = Not started

Every task starts out green, and the ones that don't perform turn yellow or red. The colors serve as a visual representation, drawing the team's attention to underserved or underperforming initiatives.

Weekly Cadence

Weekly meetings are where you will keep your rocks and 13-Week Sprint on track. In the meeting, do your best to move through the updates quickly, stopping only to discuss the tasks in yellow and red. However, when addressing these overdue items, be sure to focus on the rock or task in question rather than chastising the rock or task's owner. Ideally, owners should not be afraid to raise their hand and say, "I am struggling moving this forward. I need help." You want to build a culture that understands a rock or task being red does not mean its owner is red. Instead, work to foster a collaborative problem solving environment in which the team explores how they can help the owner get his or her rock or task back on track to green.

Tracking your organization's rocks and tasks collectively leverages public accountability. Task owners

> **YOU WANT TO BUILD A CULTURE THAT UNDERSTANDS A ROCK OR TASK BEING RED DOES NOT MEAN ITS OWNER IS RED.**

see their names on the screen with every single meeting. Taking this approach also leverages the team's collective intelligence while utilizing the problem solving strength of cross-functional groups. Ideally, the rock is put back on track within two weeks of it falling off. This is very important, as it is much easier to catch and correct problems when they are just two weeks old than when they are a full quarter behind.

Getting the two or three reds back to green with a collaborative discussion makes for a great meeting. Companies that choose to layer the updates into their normal business operations tend to continue with this process in perpetuity. However, some organizations express concern that reviewing the 13-Week Sprint is too much, too often. Use your best judgment when deciding what is right for your team.

In Appendix A, you will find a suggested weekly meeting agenda. To keep things fresh, I have created a meeting structure for the first and third weeks of the month and a different one for the second and fourth weeks of the month.

GET EVERYONE IN THE RACE

Typically, when organizations gather their leadership for a quarterly or BreakAway Move planning session, attendees emerge with a shared sense of purpose. Inspired by the opportunity to discuss the company vision, dream about the future, and work collaboratively, team members return to their positions determined to drive the mission. But energy can be challenging to sustain, and missions can be difficult to convey. As a result, many companies experience issues executing on their quarterly and BreakAway Move planning.

Organizations that struggle with losing momentum and energy typically experience this halfway through the quarter. When normal, day-to-day operations take over, team members begin falling prey to old habits. In these moments, it is important to refocus and get back on track. Just as mountain bike racers spend countless hours training their body to react instinctively to course difficulties, building organizational muscle memory also requires training, repetition, and time. If your company experiences this loss of energy, push through. Recognize the departure from the plan, learn from the mishap, and work your way back.

Conveying the new mission can also prove challenging for team members returning from planning sessions. Inspiring organizational action is nearly impossible when no one in the company besides the leadership and rock teams are connected to the plan or BreakAway Move. Moving what is often a behemoth corporate structure requires an all-hands-on-deck effort. This is where the power of the Quarterly Race Theme comes into play.

CREATE A QUARTERLY RACE THEME

For larger companies, creating a Quarterly Race Theme is one of the most powerful and transformational techniques you can use to leverage growth. Say that you and the senior team just had a great BreakAway Move planning session. Everyone is pumped up, aligned, and committed. You have your 13-Week Sprint set and are ready to go, but you notice that the core message from the sessions is not being communicated to the rest of the staff. The reality is that most your employees were not at the planning session. They did not share your experience of inspiration and are not yet on board with plan. How do you create a bridge connecting the inspiration and energy generated at the planning sessions with the rest of your company?

The power of the Quarterly Race Theme is that it helps bring the entire company on board. It helps connect those who did not attend the session with the plan. Normally, the Quarterly Race Theme is created in a way that ties the BreakAway Move or the number-one rock from that quarter to the rest of the company in a fun and engaging way. Bringing everyone into the "know" will help promote unity and ensure that teams are focused on the plan.

Quarterly Race Themes can be posted anywhere. There is almost never an issue with prospects or clients walking in and seeing evidence of progress posted publicly. Talking about a theme with an on-site prospect is a great way to close a deal. It changes the conversation from "what we do" to "how we do it" and "how we run the company." In that respect, a theme can help create new sales faster.

HAVE EMPLOYEES HELP WITH THEME TRACKING DESIGN

Once the leadership team determines the rocks for the quarter, has the 13-Week Sprint set, and identifies the number-one thing that all the employees can do together to drive the company forward, it is time to create a Quarterly Race Theme. To do this, I recommend creating a leadership team charged with coordinating theme planning and execution. The team should consist of a few employees who did not attend the planning session. Structuring the team in this way allows the rest of the company to own their part of the plan and to actively participate in getting the job done.

The Quarterly Race Theme team should be tasked with a few important objectives. First, the team must work collaboratively to create a fun and engaging theme that will help rally the entire company behind the plan. As we discussed earlier, people desire to be part of something bigger, something greater than themselves. And if the something greater is also fun, it is a win-win situation for both the company and the employee! Next, have the team identify various methods by which the plan goals may be measured. Remember, progress is only progress if you can measure the gains. Ask the team to create a simple and clear measurement so that the organization can easily follow along. This is a crucial element in ensuring that the entire company stays engaged throughout the quarter. Lastly, the Quarterly Race Theme team will need to determine goal rewards. Incentives are a powerful tool that, when leveraged correctly, can motivate employees to accomplish great challenges.

PROGRESS IS ONLY PROGRESS IF YOU CAN MEASURE THE GAINS.

Creating the Quarterly Race Theme team helps avoid an environment where leadership returns from a planning session and is faced with "selling" the company on the plan. Instead, the team members become co-owners of the plan! Also, accountability plays an important role. While the team meets to work through the outlined objectives, members will be asked to own and account for finalizing a part of theme creation, coordinating roll out, tracking progress, or communicating the results. This creates an engaging process for the entire quarter, ensuring that everyone stays focused on the plan.

EFI—QUARTERLY RACE THEME

During a planning session, the leadership team at EFI (remember them from Chapter 2?) identified a key performance indicator (KPI) that directly affected the success of their company. The team realized that if they could increase "complete and on time" (COT), it would help them win the race and be entirely set up to implement their BreakAway Move. Why was COT so important to their plan? COT was the company's metric that measures how it performs on getting the product out on time while also keeping quality at 100 percent. This was a KPI that everyone in the company could influence positively and on a weekly basis. The sales team could work on ensuring that their orders were correct, and engineering could make sure the specifications were right. Manufacturing could work to produce items exactly as instructed, and shipping could proactively take measures to improve accuracy and expediency. The actions of every single team mattered. It was clear that they all had a part in the success of the company's BreakAway Move.

To ensure that this message was understood and received by the entire company, the leadership team developed a Quarterly Race Theme. The company created an electronic football scoreboard and came up with a point system to determine the score. Every day that they exceeded their COT number, EFI won points; every day they did not, the competitor won points. At the end of the quarter, if EFI won the game, employees could choose the food trucks that would come to their quarterly all-hands meeting. The theme was so successful that they let it run an additional quarter. Not only did COT increase, but everyone in the company was also talking and thinking about COT. They understood and connected with how each employee's specific role could influence the outcome. The entire team became COT owners.

INTEGRATING THE BREAKAWAY MOVE INTO OVERALL BUSINESS PLANNING

Business planning requires massive amount of internal (and often external) resources just to keep people on track and focused on the goal. You may have planning and meeting cadences with detailed agendas already in place. You may be using one of the many available software-as-a-service platforms, or maybe your organization utilizes spreadsheets and internal processes. Regardless of the method you use to manage daily goals and activities, it is important that you take some time to integrate the BreakAway Move into your existing planning framework. Include discussion time in your meetings, ensuring that you have at least one meeting per month with the BreakAway Move as the major topic on the agenda. However, thinking and talking just a few times a year about a strategy that could double the business within three years is not enough; in fact, it is wholly insufficient. The time invested should be in line with the potential return. You can bet your competitors are thinking about the future and planning accordingly. You must do your best to be one step ahead.

For those who do not yet have any of these foundational growth tools in place, or if you are not satisfied with the tools you are presently using, Insight CXO has created something I call the Planning Map. This tool tracks everything from core values, Epic Wins, and BreakAway Moves down to quarterly goals, rocks, and themes. Think of the Planning Map as a simple, one-page business plan that helps guide your team members to maximize your current business while setting up and executing your BreakAway Move. I realize it takes time to plan, track, and communicate, but trust me; overall, it is an incredible efficiency tool. Businesses that wander about without this tool waste time gauging their next step when they could be focusing on increasing profits. What would you rather be spending your time doing?

To download the "13-Week Sprint™" worksheet, the "Quarterly Race Theme" worksheet, and the "Planning Guide," go to insightcxo.com/tools. Also see Appendix A.

THE 13 WEEK SPRINT™

Quarter:
Department:
Team:

Green: In process – On schedule
Yellow: < 5 days behind Due Date
Red: > 5 days behind Due Date
Completed: Completed

Weeks 1–13

Rock/Action/Milestone	Owner	Status	1	2	3	*	*	13
ROCK #1	*	R/Y/G/C	Start and End Dates					
*Key tasks	*	Status						
*Key tasks	*	Status						
*Key tasks	*	Status						
ROCK #2	*	R/Y/G/C	Start and End Dates					
*Key tasks	*	Status						
*Key tasks	*	Status						
*Key tasks	*	Status						
ROCK #3	*	R/Y/G/C	Start and End Dates					
*Key tasks	*	Status						
*Key tasks	*	Status						
*Key tasks	*	Status						
ROCK #4	*	R/Y/G/C	Start and End Dates					
*Key tasks	*	Status						
*Key tasks	*	Status						
*Key tasks	*	Status						

CHAPTER 9

RESILIENCE—NAVIGATING ISSUES, SETBACKS, AND CONSTRAINTS

"The real glory is being knocked to your knees and then coming back. That's real glory. That's the essence of it."

—Vince Lombardi Jr.

Within five months of turning pro, I was in the best shape of my life and crushing most of my competition. It is difficult to describe what that level of physical ability feels like, especially when experienced at forty years old. Having endless stamina was a flat-out amazing feeling, and my performances reflected how I felt. Everything was going according to my plan. Just four weeks before the mountain bike pro nationals, I was participating in a large, early-season US cup race. All the top competitors were there. I had a great start and was in the top five going into the woods; I was right where I needed to be. I executed my plan perfectly, crossed the finish line in second place, and found myself on the podium at the largest mountain bike race on the East Coast. My goal as a pro was to get at least one podium finish, and I did it! And, to top it off, I had earned enough race points to be ranked as a top-fifteen professional national racer. My sights were set just four weeks away on nationals. I could not believe how close I was to achieving my Epic Win. But, everything changed just four days later when I experienced the first of what would turn out to be two career-ending-level injuries.

THE TREE IN THE TRAIL

Charlotte, North Carolina has a great racing community. It is not uncommon to have more than two hundred racers show up on a Wednesday night. The high turnout offers a great opportunity for local racers to sneak in a race. Although I was still a bit tired from the best regional performance of my racing career the previous Sunday, I opted to join the Wednesday evening crowd and support my local team. I started the race confident, sure that I could gain an early lead and hold it all the way to the end. But instead of following up my weekend win with a midweek victory, my worst nightmare happened. While cruising at twenty miles per hour on a dogleg left turn, my left pedal hit a root on the down stroke. I should have been standing but was sitting to conserve energy. Because I entered the turn seated, the force made my rear wheel swing out ninety degrees to the right. My left hand came off the handle and I caught the grip with my wrist. I tried to get my hand back on the bar and get the rear wheel back under me, but I overcorrected. And, as fate would have it, at that very moment I found myself inches in front of a three-foot diameter oak tree.

I hit the tree, full force, on my left side. My hip and shoulder absorbed most of the impact. I did not deflect, nor did I bounce off. Strangely enough, my body seemed to come to a dead stop the instant I hit the coarse tree bark. Shawn Ulikowski, a former pro motocross racer and head engine mechanic for a top pro motocross team, was riding behind me. Shawn has witnessed some gnarly accidents in his day, but said watching me hit the tree was different. According to Shawn, it was like watching a snowball explode against a garage door. The impact left me stunned and on the ground. I knew I was not paralyzed, but I also could not move. The pain was excruciating. Finally, after what seemed like an eternity, I slid myself off the trail. My body was writhing in pain and my mind was reeling from what had just occurred; edging off the trail was all I could bring myself to do.

In the hospital, the doctors told me that I had fractured the L1 through L4 vertebrae in my lower back. Given that national championships were just four weeks away, I was crushed. This was not just a physical blow but a mental and emotional one as well. My mind was reeling. How could this have happened? This was an easy section of a trail I knew well. I had ridden past that tree at least a dozen times. This was a huge setback. But little did I know, it would not be the last.

I began training again the moment I received a shaky OK from the doctors. Determined to regain my strength and fight my way

THIS WAS NOT JUST A PHYSICAL BLOW BUT A MENTAL AND EMOTIONAL ONE AS WELL. MY MIND WAS REELING. HOW COULD THIS HAVE HAPPENED?

back to the top, I began planning immediately. My stubbornness paid off when, against all odds, I returned to racing just two months after my crash. Thanks to the support of my team and an unwavering commitment to return to racing, things seemed to be back on track. I was even in the gym training and preparing to begin my off-season strength-training program. But unfortunately, this all-is-well-with-the-world moment was short lived, as I experienced a second, more devastating injury during off-season training. My world quickly turned sideways once again.

I had been working with my strength coach, performing simple medicine ball slams, holding the ball high above my head and slamming it to the ground—something I had done countless times before in training. But this time, when I held the ball high above my head and sent it crashing to the ground, I heard a terrible sound that seemed to come from my neck. The eerie crunching sound was almost immediately followed by a searing pain in my shoulder.

Over the coming days and weeks, the severity of the injury became clearer as the pain grew in intensity. My neck became stiffer, and I began to suffer severe and shooting pains in my left arm. I could not exercise, I could not ride a bike or run, and I could barely even drive a car. The pain was debilitating, and my life seemed to come to a grinding halt.

I tried every alternative healing method you can imagine: acupuncture, yoga, massages, and more. I did everything I could to avoid surgery. However, after exhausting my search and coming up short, I gave in and met with two spinal surgeons. As I expected, the MRI results were grim. They indicated that I had a bulging disc on my C5/6 and a herniated disc at my C6/7, which was blown out enough to cause spinal cord and nerve compression. The injury was so severe that it was easily visible on the MRI. The doctors told me that if I did not get it corrected as soon as possible, I could lose the nerve. The surgeons recommended I undergo a two-level spinal fusion, a procedure that would end my racing career and likely my riding days, as well.

The surgeons' recommendation was devastating. I found myself struggling to believe that my journey to my Epic Win would end with a career-ending injury. Could this really be the end? Would

I truly never ride again? Something within me fought against the surgeon's prognosis. It may have been pure sheer will, refusing to give up on my dream, or maybe I was just being stubborn. Who knows? Regardless, I was determined to find another way. A better way. I still had my Epic Win at the forefront of my mind. It was in my head, part of my consciousness, and I was not yet ready to give up hope.

The most successful professional athletes compete with both their bodies and minds. They understand that much of the race, or game, is strategy. Basketball and football players are well known for verbally psyching out their opponents. These athletes know if they can win the mind game, the body stands little chance of success by itself. The opposite is true as well. Positive thinking and reinforcement are powerful tools that, when leveraged correctly, can inspire teams or individuals to win against all logic and odds. I needed to overcome the odds against me and win the mind game. Never riding again was not something I was willing to concede. I had to believe there was a better option somewhere out there. I just needed to find it.

Eventually, my better option came by way of a German doctor I believe to be the best spinal surgeon in the world. I found the surgeon, a pioneer in artificial disc replacement, after a lot of painstaking and defiant research. This doctor specialized in a procedure that offered a much more appealing post-surgery prognosis, and his path to healing would allow me to continue to race. It seemed like a miracle! But my celebration was soon dampened when I realized the doctor's method was not yet approved by the FDA and, as such, would not be covered by insurance. This meant that if I wanted this treatment, I would have to travel to Germany and cover the very high costs out of pocket.

Despite the costs and risks, I declined the standard US treatment recommendation. A fusion surgery or any option resulting in the end of my racing career did not seem like something supportive of my Epic Win journey. Instead, I took the calculated risk. Not doing so would have meant giving up, and giving up on my Epic Win was not an option. After a massive amount of research and what seemed to be a beyond-believable amount of logistical planning, I departed for Germany.

FROM STRENGTH TO STRATEGY

I had surgery the January following my second injury and, thankfully, it went well. I spent some time recovering in Germany and then returned to the States to continue healing. It was a long, hard, painstaking, and expensive road that, in the end, was well worth the battle. I grew more dedicated to my Epic Win and developed a level of resilience I never had before. When the odds were stacked against me, I chose to be persistent and found a way. And, most importantly, just three months after I had two discs replaced in my neck, I could race again. My calculated risk had paid off.

As excited as I was to return to racing, my body had suffered a great deal—and it showed. In April, I came in dead last in my first two races back. It was difficult to take such dismal results. If I was being honest with myself, I knew there was no way I could truly compete with other racers without being at the level of fitness I had achieved before my setbacks. I simply could not race *their* race, because they were faster than I was in my post-neck-surgery state. If I was to have any hope of holding my own against the younger competitors, I would have to be smarter. I needed to find a way to make them race *my* race, making planning and strategy even more critical.

Going into my third race, I noticed that I felt stronger than I had in the first two races and hoped that trajectory would continue. Before the race, I spent time practicing my starts so I could control my position when I entered the woods. It worked; I made it into the woods first! During the technical sections, where it is difficult to pass, I slowed the race down enough to recover but kept the pace just fast enough so no one could pass me. On the open, fast areas, I let one or two riders get around me so I could tuck in right behind them, draft, and conserve energy, but I passed them again before the course became tight or technical. Again, I slowed the race down. I repeated this method for the full race, and it paid off. Amazingly, I ended up sprinting in for the win in the last five seconds.

LEARNING CONTROL

My BreakAway Move here was to slow down the race by more than four minutes compared to the previous winning time of races with identical trail and weather conditions. This was a great example of how the fastest rider did not win—the smartest rider won by using good race strategy.

> **MY BREAKAWAY MOVE HERE WAS TO SLOW DOWN THE RACE BY MORE THAN FOUR MINUTES COMPARED TO THE PREVIOUS WINNING TIME OF RACES WITH IDENTICAL TRAIL AND WEATHER CONDITIONS.**

As an older professional who does not recover as fast as younger competitors, this mind-set and technique changed the way I would race forever. It probably even gave me a few more years of racing at the pro level, being able to compete with some of the best young racers in the country.

CONVERTING ISSUES, SETBACKS, AND CHALLENGES INTO LEARNING

Often, the most devastating setbacks are those that seem to evade reason and logic. Crashing into a tree while riding through a turn seated when I should have been standing, although frustrating, made some logical sense. It was a handling error. The mistake was a tangible moment of lax judgment that resulted in a serious crash and a precise moment I could point to and attempt to correct in the future. But the second injury was different and challenged me in a way I had never experienced.

Issues, problems, constraints, and setbacks will inevitably happen in both business and life. Some things you see coming, like the tree in the trail, while other challenges can sneak up on you. Then, without warning or notice, you find yourself deep in a struggle. When this happens, our instincts are to fight as hard as we can to change our circumstances as quickly as possible. However, as a lifelong entrepreneur and a coach to high-growth companies, I have learned that some of the biggest lessons and gains come when we thoughtfully navigate through problems and setbacks. As a company leader, the only truly "bad" problems are the ones you don't know about and the ones you choose to ignore. If you choose to approach a challenge with an open mind and a willingness to learn, you and the company will be better for it.

Great leaders build resilient teams that can consistently and successfully navigate through issues. As a result, these teams become stronger over time. Adversity can create environments where a team produces their best work. If everything is easy, there is no reason to really focus and draw on your creative muscle. Muscles that go unused for a long period of time can become weak and atrophied. The same is true for our mind. Engaging your creative intellect to think your way out of a challenge is great brain exercise. When new issues or challenges occur, they are more like stimuli that focus the team and energize its members.

Working on issues each week should be a normal habit. In fact, it should be unusual to *not* work on issues. Being intentional about working on problems does not mean you are being negative; it simply means you are being realistic. Do this enough, and your organization will develop a level of resilience superior to any of your competitors. As your team attacks challenges and ultimately overcomes them, they will become leaner, stronger, and smarter than you ever imagined.

ISSUES AND SETBACKS

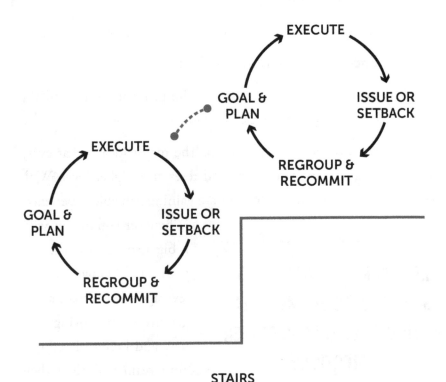

STAIRS

Jim Collins, *Good to Great: Why Some Companies Make the Leap... and Others Don't* (HarperBusiness, 2011).

Setbacks are just lessons and opportunities waiting to happen. You have a choice to learn and improve, or complain and quit. When I am working with clients, I take advantage of any issues or setbacks that occur. When they do, it presents a fantastic opportunity to reveal a valuable lesson and get them thinking about something in a new way. As Jim Collins so famously said in his book *Good to Great*, "Good is the enemy of great." My experience is that if things are just good, it is hard to make change happen. Sometimes a setback is exactly what is needed to motivate and move the team in the right direction.

Progress is never linear, in anything we do—inside or outside of work. There are four parts to the natural cycle of progress:

1. Committing to a project or goal

2. Doing the work and creating progress and achievement

3. Encountering an issue or setback

4. Learning, brainstorming, coaching, recommitting to the goal, and getting back to progress

This process continues in a loop. The major idea is that every time a setback occurs, you adapt and reset at a higher level. With every challenge, you and your team are gaining valuable experience.

Whenever you get hit with a big issue or setback, ask yourself, "How can I leverage this situation to get my team moving in a new and better direction?" Your team will be at their most coachable at this point, so do not squander

> **HOW CAN I LEVERAGE THIS SITUATION TO GET MY TEAM MOVING IN A NEW AND BETTER DIRECTION?**

the opportunity. Although I never want clients to have big issues, part of me becomes excited when a challenge arises. Why? Because as a coach, I want to see you and your team improve, and because I know that hyper-growth companies share a unique ability to experience challenges and setbacks and learn from them. They don't ask for problems, but when problems occur, they don't shy away.

BreakAway Moves will be riddled with problems. Assumptions that were made early on, with limited information, will invariably return a different result, and the team will need to learn and adapt. During times of adversity, your company needs a mechanism, a culture, and a cadence to keep the momentum high. Meetings that focus solely on updates are boring. Keep a rolling list of problems, issues, and opportunities and discuss them as a group. There should never be a shortage of juicy and interesting topics for your team to discuss. I recommend a weekly cadence, preferably in the form of a weekly meeting, where these issues are discussed along with action plans for working through and solving them. As the team works through the list, they will become smarter, stronger, and more independent. And before you know it, they will have a strong and healthy ability to work through their challenges, even in the CEO's absence.

THE POWER OF CONSTRAINTS

Often, people do their best work with constraints. Constraints come in infinite forms, and you never really know when they will present themselves. You want your team centered on getting into the

> YOU WANT YOUR TEAM CENTERED ON GETTING INTO THE MIND-SET AND HABIT OF LOOKING FOR CONSTRAINTS.

mind-set and habit of looking for constraints, as these are opportunities to improve. Some challenges can be solved in short periods of time, some take longer, and some may prove impossible to overcome. But instead of complaining, just acknowledge a constraint for what it is and get to work using your collective intelligence to identify a workaround.

Creating artificial constraints when planning or running meetings can serve to stimulate the creative juices and prompt innovative thinking. How can we launch a new idea without spending more than *x* dollars to get it started? How can we do this without personally working any overtime? How can we do this without taking on outside investment or debt? Can we change our one-hour meetings to forty-five minutes without losing human connection? Layering in the constraints will challenge your team's ability to adapt, and they will become better at it over time, producing some genius workarounds. This should be a primary focus for your team.

The world will throw problems your way, and it is important that we adapt quickly and continue on our path despite the challenges. This is true in business and in life. I learned this lesson firsthand while racing professionally. When setbacks occurred, I had to battle through. When injuries created performance constraints, I had to adapt and find a way to win despite the tree in the trail.

IN BUSINESS, YOU WANT TO CREATE A CULTURE AND PROCESS THAT ALMOST CELEBRATES PROBLEMS, OR AT LEAST THE SHARING OF THEM.

CREATE A CULTURE OF SHARING PROBLEMS

In business, you want to create a culture and process

that almost celebrates problems, or at least the sharing of them. Most managers shy away from sharing problems for fear of being reprimanded for inferior performance. This is a shame; think of all the learning opportunities missed because of fear. Leaning into problems and celebrating the learning they offer sounds counterintuitive, but it is critical.

Getting the right team on board is essential to your company's success. The team needs to have complete trust in one another so that they can be vulnerable, sharing their departments' problems. If trust is present, the teams can discuss and debate issues, eventually identifying the best solutions. Of the companies I have worked with, almost every one that experienced a significant problem or constraint has gone on to have a successful breakout performance. In every case, they could trace their new, successful strategy back to some type of pain or serious challenge. When coaching clients, I am a heat-seeking missile for issues and problems. I do whatever I can to get the team to let those things come to the surface. I want to see a breakout occur, and I know facing problems is the best way to accomplish that.

I WANT TO SEE A BREAKOUT OCCUR, AND I KNOW FACING PROBLEMS IS THE BEST WAY TO ACCOMPLISH THAT.

When I founded Insight CXO, several people offered me seed capital. They were betting on the rider, not the bike. I said, "No thank you," to all of them, because the reality is that I do better with constraints. I knew Insight CXO would become a stronger company, and faster, if I experienced constraints in the beginning.

AVIDXCHANGE—WINNING WITH CONSTRAINTS

I cofounded AvidXchange in 2000. It was an early software-as-a-service company, created to revolutionize the way real estate investment trusts and owners of large commercial real estate assets bought supplies and services to maintain their properties. The concept was to build an online exchange where commercial real estate buyers and suppliers could buy and sell using reverse-auction technology. The idea was to drive down prices while also exposing suppliers to more opportunities—a win-win.

We raised a little more than $1 million in start-up capital. This may sound modest, but considering it was right after the stock market crash and dot-com bust, it was especially difficult to do at that time. But our three major competitors had raised more than $50 million just before the crash. At real estate trade shows, they had huge, no-expense-spared, hundred-by-hundred-foot booths in corner locations, while we were stuck in a ten-by-ten-foot booth with a used display and a vinyl banner displaying our logo. Before long, we were hit with a huge setback we could not have seen coming: Clarus, the public company that sold us the software platform on which we ran the online exchange, ran out of cash and shut down. Clarus was a casualty of the dot-com bust, and unfortunately, we were collateral damage.

With Clarus out of the picture, we were on our own for software support. The unexpected turn of events may have crushed a less resilient company, but surprisingly, this setback created our first great strategic pivot. Under the amazing leadership of Chris Tinsley, AvidXchange cofounder and chief technology officer, we transitioned our software platform from being an online exchange business to managing invoices and payment processes for real estate investment trusts and their suppliers. Chris built an in-house development team to create the software from scratch, and suddenly we had control over our own destiny. Companies that face challenges head-on, capitalize on setbacks, and leverage learning are poised for greatness.

RACING AT NATIONALS

The pro courses almost always go straight up a mountain, usually up a ski slope, and then zigzag their way back down through the trees to the start. The day before I raced in the pro mountain bike nationals in Sun Valley, Idaho, I was practicing on one of the super tricky downhill switchbacks when I saw Todd Wells, the previous year's champion and winner of the coveted stars and stripes jersey, just crushing it up the seemingly vertical mountain climb. For perspective, the climb is so steep that if you lose traction and stall, it's nearly impossible to get restarted; it's hike-a-bike to the top! Just watching Todd grind up the mountain and reflecting back on everything it took for me to get there, I felt like I had already achieved the impossible. At that moment, all that I had done and accomplished suddenly became *real*.

The day of the race seemed beyond surreal. I can remember sitting on my bike, waiting for the start, lined up with fifty of the fastest guys in the United States. Thousands of people were lined up along the course, ringing cowbells and making all kinds of noise. Once the starting gun went off, we raced around the ski lodge, tore through a nasty, hundred-plus-foot, man-made rock garden, and started the grueling climb to the top of the course. I made it around four times, passing about ten other riders, when out of nowhere, a setback hit. The sidewall of my tire got sliced on my downhill run to the base of the mountain, and my race was immediately over. I was a bit frustrated but, surprisingly, not upset. And rather than make my way down into the noisy crowd of spectators, I decided to stay right where I was. I stood back and watched the race leaders battle it out for the stars and stripes jersey while I felt full of life, having achieved my Epic Win. I was there; I had made it!

To download the "Issues, Setback, and Constraints Breakthrough™" worksheet, go to insightcxo.com/tools. Also see Appendix A.

THE ISSUES, SETBACKS AND CONSTRAINTS BREAK THROUGH™

WORKSHEET PURPOSE:

To provide a structure to navigate through problems in a healthy and consistent manner with a result that makes your company stronger.

Describe the issue, setback or constraint you'd like to grow from
*

Describe what the ideal result would have been:
*

What worked?	What did not work?
*	*

Knowing what you know now, what would you do differently?
*

What are the steps you will take to avoid this problem or solve it faster in the future?
1.
2.
3.
4.
5.

CHAPTER 10

START TO FINISH—SET THE PACE TO WIN THE RACE

"If you go to work on your goals, your goals will go to work on you. If you go to work on your plan, your plan will go to work on you. Whatever good things we build end up building us."

—Jim Rohn

Creating, developing, and implementing your company's BreakAway Move is not a fast or simple process. A BreakAway Move is something no one else in your industry has done or even considered doing, so by definition it should not be something that can happen overnight. It should be something that takes considerable energy, time, effort, and focus to make it happen. You are launching your company out of the pack and into the lead. Nothing about that is fast or simple.

PACING, PASSING, AND BREAKING YOUR OPPONENT'S RHYTHM

As I have said various times throughout this book, two of the most important aspects of this process are cadence and pacing. When you are in a mountain bike race and have a long, big hill to climb, you don't go up the hill at 100 percent the entire time. If you attempted to climb at that pace, you would wear yourself out early. Instead, you pace yourself and go maybe 90 percent until you near the top. Then, at that point, you pick up your speed and push to 100 percent. This will carry you faster and more efficiently down the other side. You might have to climb a hundred hills in a two-hour race, and racing smart can shave minutes off your total time. It is all about *how* you spend your energy.

Finally, once you've set your pace and know when and where you are going to pass, you will need to determine how you can break your competitors' rhythm. If you have ever watched the Tour de France, you may have seen a rider break away from the front of the pack when they are going up a mountain. We call that "the attack." Often, when a rider attempts an attack, the group just pulls them right back in. As a viewer this can be confusing, and you may even wonder, "Why is this person just attacking and attacking over again?" It may seem pointless, but I can tell you that the rider is skillfully executing a strategy. Essentially, the rider is trying to break the leaders in the group so that they begin to "crack" and become unable to maintain the pace and accelerations any longer. The person breaking away is disrupting the rhythm of the group. In business, I like to say the universe is constantly "attacking" the

---

WHATEVER IT IS, THERE WILL ALWAYS BE DISRUPTIONS AND ATTACKS ON YOUR RHYTHM. FIGHT THEM. DO NOT LET THEM MAKE YOU CRACK. PROTECT YOUR CADENCE, AND KEEP ON MARCHING TOWARD YOUR BREAKAWAY MOVE.

---

company through macroeconomic factors, internal issues, production problems, huge amounts of new business at once, and so on. Whatever it is, there will always be disruptions and attacks on your rhythm. Fight them. Do not let them make you crack. Protect your cadence, and keep on marching toward your BreakAway Move.

THE RACE PLAN: CREATING YOUR WINNING PLAN

You may be wondering where to start or how to facilitate this with your team. To help with this, I created a step-by-step process that will guide you through implementing the concepts. When I race, it is common for my lap times to get faster rather than slower. Although I become more fatigued, I am learning the course, figuring out the competition, and determining the best line to help me go faster with less energy. I am constantly improving. Creating and implementing your BreakAway Move will work much the same way.

The process is structured in laps, much like a race. In each lap, you become more efficient in each section, and everything is easier and has more flow to it. You continue with this process until, in the final lap, you have your BreakAway Move all set and ready for execution with your team. The process intentionally repeats, because that is the best way to master the concepts and iterate on your previous work. And you and your team will retain more and improve faster. For example, working on core values over several weeks is more powerful than one marathon session. Each time your team circles back on a topic, they see it in a new way and can apply it to their daily work lives more effectively.

I've included a checklist that serves as a general guide for building your company's BreakAway Move. If you are already on an annual, quarterly, and monthly planning rhythm, just integrate this checklist into your existing meeting agendas. If you need help in establishing good meeting rhythms, go to the Insight CXO website and download our meeting agendas. But when using the checklist, keep in mind that the objective is not to just check the boxes. You use the checklist so that the components begin to stick.

STARTING LINE

Have your team read *The BreakAway Move* and set a half- or full-day planning session in advance.

LAP 1

- **Create your core values in draft form**. Download "The Intentional Culture" worksheet from the website.

- **Create your core purpose in draft form.** Download the "Energy Secret: Core Purpose" worksheet from the website.

- **Create your company's Epic Win in draft form**. Download the "Epic Win Creator" worksheet from the website.

- **Get your leadership team above the tree line and thinking globally**. Download and complete the "SWeaT—Strengths, Weaknesses, and Trends" worksheet from the website.

- **Complete the Planning Map in draft form**. Download "The BreakAway Move Planning Map" worksheet from the website. Take a first pass at filling in all the boxes so you can start seeing the puzzle come together. Focus on the annual priorities and getting the quarterly rocks right.

- **Complete the first 13-Week Sprint**. Download "The 13-Week Sprint" worksheet from the website. Take the rocks from the Planning Map and transfer them to the 13-Week Sprint document for execution. Using a Google Sheets version of the 13-Week Sprint is highly recommended because of the collaboration capability built into Google Sheets. Send us an e-mail, and we will share a prebuilt 13-Week Sprint file with you.

- **Create or integrate BreakAway Move meeting cadences and agendas.** If you need help with this, download sample daily, weekly, monthly, quarterly, and annual meeting agendas from the website.

LAP 2

- **Finalize your core values, core purpose, and Epic Win.** Include communication plans for the rest of the company.

- **Determine the revenue difference between where your current business will take you compared to your five-year revenue targets.** Download and complete the "Five-Year Targets—Define the Revenue Gap" worksheet from the website.

- **Define who your core customers are or will be, and create your brand promise(s).** Download and complete the "Brand Promise—Define Your Target Audience" and "Brand Promise—Taking Control of Your Growth" worksheets from the website.

- **Create a list of five to fifteen BreakAway Move candidate ideas.** Use questions from the book, or download the "BreakAway Move Questions" worksheet from the website.

- **Start creating Role-Alignment Cards (RACe) for the leadership team.** Download "The Role-Alignment Card™ Advantage" from the website.

- **Update the Planning Map and 13-Week Sprint.**

- **Get the full company aligned around what is most important for the next quarter.** Download "The Quarterly Race Theme" from the website.

LAP 3

- **Complete Role-Alignment Cards for the leadership team** and create a plan to roll them out to all the major roles in the company.

- **Prioritize the top three BreakAway Moves** and start aligning and preparing resources. Get action items and tasks down to the 13-Week Sprint for execution and accountability. Download "The BreakAway Move Evaluator" from the website.

- **Finalize the brand promise(s)** and start operational implementation and tuning. Update the Planning Map.

- **Create a "Team #1" mind-set.** Start working with your senior team to make sure they can trust each other and can learn put the overall needs of the senior team ahead of their individual departments.

- **Establish communication cadence.** Work on full-company communications systems and processes that facilitate the free flow of information up and down the organization. Can everyone in the company articulate the Epic Win? Do all employees know the key behaviors supporting the core values?

- **Continue updating and adjusting the Planning Map and 13-Week Sprint.** Nail down the top BreakAway Move and make sure you have the right energy, time, and money to support it.

- **Create a culture that leverages issues, problems, and setbacks.** Start choosing at least one issue each week for the team to work on together. Download the "Issues, Setbacks, and Constraints Breakthrough™" worksheet from the website.

- **Update the Planning Map and 13-Week Sprint.**

WORKSHEETS

This Appendix includes the worksheets that were mentioned throughout the book. Rather than including the worksheets in the chapters and interrupting the flow of the book, I have included them all in one place for easy reference. These worksheets, which I refer to as "workouts" in my sessions with clients, were created as mechanisms or tools to engage your team with new ways of thinking. All the worksheets ultimately build up to the Planning Map and 13-Week Sprint, which are the foundational documents that help drive visibility, accountability, and ultimately BreakAway Move results.

I recommend using the implementation plan I outline in Chapter 10, but feel free to pick the worksheet that can address an immediate pain. Is morale lower than you would like, and you have a big obstacle in your way? Go to the "Power of Issues and Setbacks" worksheet first. Then circle back, work on your strong core, and progress from there.

The Insight CXO website will have full and complete downloadable versions of the worksheets that you can use with your teams. I add new worksheets, facilitation guides, and real end-user experiences to my blog each month, so make sure you sign up on the website for content updates.

THE ENERGY SECRET—CORE PURPOSE™

WORKSHEET PURPOSE:

To identify what really gets the company motivated to accomplish great things. Answers the why we do what we do question.

DESCRIPTION STATEMENT "WHAT DOES YOUR COMPANY DO?"

_____

_____

1. WHY IS THIS IMPORTANT?

_____

_____

    2. WHY DOES THIS MATTER?

    _____

    _____

        3. WHY IS THIS IMPORTANT?

        _____

        _____

            4. WHY DOES THIS MATTER?

            _____

            _____

                5. WHY IS THIS IMPORTANT?

                _____

                _____

OUR CORE PURPOSE: _____

    Hints: _Keep this as a short phrase so it's easy to remember._
              You don't have to go 5 deep on the Why's. If #3 resonates, use it.

              Do this first in draft from and circle back until it feels right.

IDEAS AND NOTES

What ideas or insights come into mind right now looking at this worksheet?

What would the impact be of having the team work together on this?

When should I discuss and/or implement this with the team?

How will I facilitate this?

Who needs to be a part of the exercise?

How will I make sure insights and decisions stick?

INTENTIONAL CULTURE–CORE VALUES™

WORKSHEET PURPOSE:

To identify and name the core behaviors that define the culture and character of the business.

WHO Names of real people inside the organization

1.   4.

2.   5.

3.

Hint: High credibility with peers. Most competent in their roles. Would re-hire this type of person. Positive role models.

WHY Significant attributes or characteristics of the people you selected.

1.   4.

2.   5.

3.

Examples: Trustworthy; Work Ethic; Team Player; Caring; Learner: Open minded; Passionate; Problem Solver; Results Driven

CORE VALUE DEFINITION:	Small set of timeless principles. Standards vs. rules.
	Internally focused. Intrinsic value and importance.
	Independent of type of business you are in.
CORE VALUE TEST:	Must exist within at least one person, preferably majority of the company.
	Must be willing to take a financial hit to protect.
	Must be willing to fire a multiple offender.
	Internal or external.
OUR CORE VALUES:	1.
	2.
	3.
	4.
	5.

IDEAS AND NOTES

What ideas or insights come into mind right now looking at this worksheet?

What would the impact be of having the team work together on this?

When should I discuss and/or implement this with the team?

How will I facilitate this?

Who needs to be a part of the exercise?

How will I make sure insights and decisions stick?

EPIC WIN CREATOR™

WORKSHEET PURPOSE:

To create a significant 10 year goal for the business that creates clarity on company direction and gets everyone aligned and excited.

Step 1 What are the Inherent Strengths or Core Competencies in the business? What are you best in the world at?

1.   4.
2.   5.
3.

Step 2 What drives your economic engine? What drives your revenue and profit?

1.   4.
2.   5.
3.

Step 3 What does your team get energized about? What drives the passion to do the work you do? What is your Core Purpose?

1.   4.
2.   5.
3.

Step 4 Combine the top statements from each category above and create a short phrase Epic Win.

1.   4.
2.   5.
3.

Hint: Epic Win's can be stated different ways. Most common are Inspirational, Competitive, Humanitarian and Core Purpose

Step 5 Make sure your Epic Win is measurable. How will you keep score along the way? What are the measures, KPI's?.

1.
2.
3.

IDEAS AND NOTES

What ideas or insights come into mind right now looking at this worksheet?

What would the impact be of having the team work together on this?

When should I discuss and/or implement this with the team?

How will I facilitate this?

Who needs to be a part of the exercise?

How will I make sure insights and decisions stick?

THE ROLE ALIGNMENT CARD™

WORKSHEET PURPOSE:

To create a benchmark for each role with vision to the full company goals/objectives and also providing clarity accountability, and success factors. Each person should know how to win.

Title:

Role Objective:

Accountabilities	Priority	% of Time	Success Measures/Goals
*	(1–5)	%	*
*	(1–5)	%	*
*	(1–5)	%	*
*	(1–5)	%	*
*	(1–5)	%	*

Core Competencies and Skills	
1	*
2	*
3	*
4	*
5	*
6	*
7	*

Company Core Values	How the Core Value Relates Specifically to the Role
*	*
*	*
*	*
*	*
*	*

IDEAS AND NOTES

What ideas or insights come into mind right now looking at this worksheet?

What would the impact be of having the team work together on this?

When should I discuss and/or implement this with the team?

How will I facilitate this?

Who needs to be a part of the exercise?

How will I make sure insights and decisions stick?

5 YEAR TARGETS—DEFINING THE REVENUE GAP

WORKSHEET PURPOSE:

To determine where the revenue GAPs are based on current offerings or growth strategy.

	Year 1	Year 2	Year 3	Year 4	Year 5
REVENUE TARGET					
Current Product/Service					
Current Product/Service					
Current Product/Service					
Current Product/Service					
Current Product/Service					
TOTAL REV CURRENT PRODUCT/SERVICE					
REVENUE GAP = TARGET - CURRENT					
BreakAway Move #1 Rev Projection					
BreakAway Move #2 Rev Projection					
BreakAway Move #3 Rev Projection					
TOTAL BREAKAWAY MOVE PROJECTION					
ACTION ITEMS:	**TOP 3 THINGS TO START ADDRESSING THE GAP**				
1					
2					
3					

IDEAS AND NOTES

What ideas or insights come into mind right now looking at this worksheet?

What would the impact be of having the team work together on this?

When should I discuss and/or implement this with the team?

How will I facilitate this?

Who needs to be a part of the exercise?

How will I make sure insights and decisions stick?

SWeaT—STRENGTHS, WEAKNESS AND TRENDS

WORKSHEET PURPOSE:

To get the team above the tree line and in the right mindset for Strategy discussions.

Global Trends
What are the significant trends going on in the world around us? What are the advancements in technology distributions systems, marketing, social media, business models, industry specific changes that could impact the business?

Inherent Strengths/Core Competencies
What are the things that your company has been able to hone over the years and is a source of your success? What do you do better than anyone else? What are you exceptionally good at?

Inherent Weakness
What are the weaknesses or significant constraints that are not easily changed? All weakness can be overcome over time, focus on what can't be easily changed in the next 1–2 years.

Hint: Spend the most time on Trends. Most teams do not spend enough time discussing the world around them.

IDEAS AND NOTES

What ideas or insights come into mind right now looking at this worksheet?

What would the impact be of having the team work together on this?

When should I discuss and/or implement this with the team?

How will I facilitate this?

Who needs to be a part of the exercise?

How will I make sure insights and decisions stick?

THE CORE CUSTOMER FOCUS™

WORKSHEET PURPOSE:
To define WHO and WHERE the Brand Promise will be created for.

Core Customer
Create a Buyer Persona based on real clients who: Buy for optimal profit, you want more of, say please and thank you, who refer you to others, and see you as a partner.

List names of REAL clients	List the matching key attribute	Short description of your Core Customer
*	*	*
*	*	
*	*	
*	*	
*	*	

Define Your Area of Play – Sandbox
Decide roughly what your 3 year revenue target is going to be. What do you need to dominate to hit your 3 year revenue target? Should be large enough to hit your target and small enough to stay focused. These are demographics, geographics, business lines, channels will you sell through, verticals/horizontals, etc.

List of Attributes	List of Attributes	Short description of your Sandbox
*	*	*
*	*	
*	*	
*	*	
*	*	

IDEAS AND NOTES

What ideas or insights come into mind right now looking at this worksheet?

What would the impact be of having the team work together on this?

When should I discuss and/or implement this with the team?

How will I facilitate this?

Who needs to be a part of the exercise?

How will I make sure insights and decisions stick?

BRAND PROMISE–TAKING CONTROL OF YOUR GROWTH

WORKSHEET PURPOSE:

To create a unique Brand Promise that magnetizes your Core Customer to your company and repels the rest. Creates a meaningful platform to tune your operations and differentiate form competition.

BRAND PROMISE REQUIREMENTS:

Must fill a client NEED and not just a want.	Must differentiate you.
Must be hard to do. Hard to replicate by competition.	Must be measurable by you and your clients.
It must encourage your Core Customer to take action sooner.	Typically 1 lead Promise and 2 supporting Promises.

CREATING THE BRAND PROMISE:

Core Competencies	Core Customer Need	Competitors Offerings
*	*	*
*	*	*
*	*	*
*	*	*
*	*	*

Based on the lists above, what are your Core Competencies AND Core Customer Needs that the Competition does not offer? Refer back to the Requirements definition.

CREATING 3 BRAND PROMISE:

Primary/Lead	*
Supporting	*
Supporting	*

IDEAS AND NOTES

What ideas or insights come into mind right now looking at this worksheet?

What would the impact be of having the team work together on this?

When should I discuss and/or implement this with the team?

How will I facilitate this?

Who needs to be a part of the exercise?

How will I make sure insights and decisions stick?

THE 13 WEEK SPRINT™

Quarter:

Department:

Team:

Green: In process – On schedule

Yellow: < 5 days behind Due Date

Red: > 5 days behind Due Date

Completed: Completed

Weeks 1–13

Rock/Action/Milestone	Owner	Status	1	2	3	*	*	13
ROCK #1	*	R/Y/G/C	Start and End Dates					
*Key tasks	*	Status						
*Key tasks	*	Status						
*Key tasks	*	Status						

Rock/Action/Milestone	Owner	Status	1	2	3	*	*	13
ROCK #2	*	R/Y/G/C	Start and End Dates					
*Key tasks	*	Status						
*Key tasks	*	Status						
*Key tasks	*	Status						

Rock/Action/Milestone	Owner	Status	1	2	3	*	*	13
ROCK #3	*	R/Y/G/C	Start and End Dates					
*Key tasks	*	Status						
*Key tasks	*	Status						
*Key tasks	*	Status						

Rock/Action/Milestone	Owner	Status	1	2	3	*	*	13
ROCK #4	*	R/Y/G/C	Start and End Dates					
*Key tasks	*	Status						
*Key tasks	*	Status						
*Key tasks	*	Status						

IDEAS AND NOTES

What ideas or insights come into mind right now looking at this worksheet?

What would the impact be of having the team work together on this?

When should I discuss and/or implement this with the team?

How will I facilitate this?

Who needs to be a part of the exercise?

How will I make sure insights and decisions stick?

THE ISSUES, SETBACKS AND CONSTRAINTS BREAK THROUGH™

WORKSHEET PURPOSE:

To provide a structure to navigate through problems in a healthy and consistent manner with a result that makes your company stronger.

Describe the issue, setback or constraint you'd like to grow from
*

Describe what the ideal result would have been:
*

What worked?	What did not work?
*	*

Knowing what you know now, what would you do differently?
*

What are the steps you will take to avoid this problem or solve it faster in the future?
1.
2.
3.
4.
5.

IDEAS AND NOTES

What ideas or insights come into mind right now looking at this worksheet?

What would the impact be of having the team work together on this?

When should I discuss and/or implement this with the team?

How will I facilitate this?

Who needs to be a part of the exercise?

How will I make sure insights and decisions stick?

MEETING CADENCE AND STRUCTURE

Getting into a strong communication rhythm with your team is vital for both BreakAway Move creation and execution. There are four primary roles in each meeting and, preferably, are not all covered by the CEO and are four different people. Each meeting needs a leader, someone who can make final decisions if the group can't reach a consensus on a topic. Each meeting needs a facilitator, someone who can help keep the group focused on the agenda and outcomes. Each meeting needs time keeper, someone who can make sure the agenda is covered and makes the group aware when topics take the team too far off track. Finally, each meeting needs a scribe who can keep track of what decisions were made, what actions were promised, by when, and by whom. A fifth role can be added as well and is one of my personal favorites. I call it the parking lot attendant. This person is listening to the overall conversations during the meeting and records key issues or ideas that come up but are not discussed. This is a great way to come up with topics to discuss in future tactical meetings. The parking lot attendant can also help keep the meeting running smoothly by preventing an off topic discussion from taking too much time. They can stop the conversation, write down the topic, and then address it at the end of the meeting.

TEAM MEETINGS

Daily Huddle	Daily	< 15 Minutes	All Team Members
Bi-Weekly (Tactical)	1st &3 rd Week	60 minutes	All Team Members and/or Leadership
Bi-Weekly (Strategic)	2nd & 4th Week	60-90 minutes	Mid to Senior Level Leadership
Quarterly Leadership	Quarterly	4 – 8 Hours	Senior Level Leadership
Quarterly Planning	Quarterly	4 – 8 Hours	All Team Members
Annual Planning	Annual	1 – 3 Days	Mid and Senior Level Leadership with Full Team Collaboration

AGENDAS

DAILY HUDDLE

MEETING OBJECTIVES:
- o Synchronize the team
- o Uncover issues quickly for they become problems
- o Speed communication

Format: Team members should all be standing. If some team members need to be remote on a consistent basis, have everyone use their phone so everyone has the same huddle experience. Go around the room four times. Quickly!

Round 1 – What is a personal or professional win or good news since our last huddle?

Round 2 – What is your #1 priority in the next 24 hours?

Round 3 – What are your issues, stucks, frustrations, constraints, etc?

Round 4 – What are you working or doing that might impact someone else?

AGENDA

WEEKLY MEETING – Strategic (2nd and 4th week of the month)

MEETING OBJECTIVES:
- o Work on culture – Core Values, Purpose and Epic Win
- o Planning Map - Focus on BreakAway Move strategy, Priorities, Rocks and review the Planning Map
- o Decision Making – Use collective intelligence of the team to brainstorm and make any adjustments to the Planning Map and 13 Week Sprint. Make decisions on one or two key issues.

3 Minutes   **Open Meeting**
Review agenda and any special announcements

5 Minutes   **Core Values, Purpose and Epic Win**
Share stories from the last two weeks – look for opportunities and issues

10 Minutes   **Data**
Review company and departmental metrics and KPI's

30 Minutes   **Review Quarterly Rocks and 13 Week Sprint**
Green – Yellow – Red status on all tasks
Discuss BreakAway Moves and company strategy

5 Minutes   **Feedback**
Review and discuss any employee and/or customer feedback. Identify opportunities and issues to be addressed.

7 Minutes   **Close – Review**
- o Decisions Made
- o Who, What and When for adjustments and actions
- o Decide cascading communication
- o Address Parking Lot

AGENDA

WEEKLY MEETING – Tactical (1st and 3rd week of the month)

MEETING OBJECTIVES:

- Stay Focused – work on tactical and day-to-day issues that must be addressed
- Stay Connected – on what's most important
- Decision Making – Use collective intelligence of the team to brainstorm, then make decisions on one or two key issues, opportunities or challenges.

10 Minutes	**Lightning Round (1 minute per person)** Each person shares: 2 most important priorities / rocks / BreakAway Moves they/their team is working on for the next two weeks; 1 team issue they feel must be discussed:
4 Minutes	**Pause** Evaluate and choose 3 most important issues facing the team/organization that must be discussed today, discuss below:
13 Minutes	**Discuss Topic #1** Present Issue – Ask questions – Brainstorm solutions – Who What When next steps
13 Minutes	**Discuss Topic #1** Present Issue – Ask questions – Brainstorm solutions – Who What When next steps
13 Minutes	**Discuss Topic #1** Present Issue – Ask questions – Brainstorm solutions – Who What When next steps
7 Minutes	**Close – Review** ○ Decisions Made ○ Who, What and When for adjustments and actions ○ Decide cascading communication ○ Address Parking Lot

9 781599 325989